C

ESSAYS ON HER WORKS

WRITERS SERIES 2
SERIES EDITORS:
ANTONIO D'ALFONSO AND JOSEPH PIVATO

Canadä

Guernica Editions Inc. acknowledges the support of The Canada Council for the Arts.
Guernica Editions Inc. acknowledges the support of the Ontario Arts Council.
Guernica Editions Inc. acknowledges the financial support of the Government of Canada through the Book Publishing Industry Development Program (BPIDP).

CATERINA EDWARDS

ESSAYS ON HER WORKS

EDITED BY JOSEPH PIVATO

GUERNICA
TORONTO•BUFFALO•LANCASTER (U.K.)
2000

Copyright © 2000, by Joseph Pivato
and Guernica Editions Inc.
All rights reserved. The use of any part of this publication,
reproduced, transmitted in any form or by any means,
electronic, mechanical, photocopying, recording or otherwise
stored in a retrieval system, without the prior consent of the
publisher is an infringement of the copyright law.

Guernica Editions Inc.
P.O. Box 117, Station P, Toronto (ON), Canada M5S 2S6
2250 Military Road, Tonawanda, N.Y. 14150-6000 U.S.A.
Gazelle, Falcon House, Queen Square,
Lancaster LA1 1RN U.K.
Typeset by Selina.
Printed in Canada.

Legal Deposit – Second Quarter
National Library of Canada
Library of Congress Catalog Card Number: 00-101688

Canadian Cataloguing in Publication Data
Caterina Edwards : essays on her works
(Writers series ; 2)
Includes bibliographical references.
ISBN 1-55071-114-8
1. Edwards, Caterina. – Criticism and interpretation.
I. Pivato, Joseph. II. Series: Writers series (Toronto, Ont.); 2.
PS8559.D83Z62   2000   C818'.5409   C00-900535-8
PR9199.3.E364Z62   2000

Table of Contents

Acknowledgements	6
Introduction: A Marriage of Life and Art	
by Joseph Pivato	7
Entrapped Women: Edwards' Short Stories	
by Elizabeth Sarlo-Hayes	19
Edmonton Versus Venice: The Whole Truth	
by Petra Fachinger	39
The Social Construction of Subjectivity in Edwards'	
The Lion's Mouth by Marino Tuzi	56
Cinderella Revisioned: The Female Persona in Caterina	
Edwards, Genni Gunn, and Mary di Michele	
by Frank Caucci	83
Research Notes on Edwards' Fiction	
by Pasquale Verdicchio	97
A Shote Note on *Becoming Emma*	
by Anna Pia De Luca	101
Dialogue: Caterina Edwards and Jacqueline Dumas	105
Brief Biography of Caterina Edwards	119
Bibliography: Works by and about Caterina Edwards	122
List of Contributors	126

Acknowledgements

The editor would like to thank the following for making this volume possible: The authors and Guernica Editions for permission to use excerpts from the following books: Marino Tuzi, *The Power of Allegiances* (1997) and Pasquale Verdicchio, *Devils in Paradise* (1997); the contributors: Frank Caucci, Anna Pia De Luca, Jacqueline Dumas, Petra Fachinger, Elizabeth Sarlo-Hayes, and Caterina Edwards. "A Short Note on *Becoming Emma*" is taken from *Are There Ghosts in Italian-Canadian Female Writing?* By Anna Pia De Luca (Università di Bologna, September 1999). I would personally like to thank Antonio D'Alfonso for his support and Emma Pivato for her encouragement.

Introduction

Marriage of Life and Art

JOSEPH PIVATO

In the Atom Egoyan film, *Calendar*, the Canadian photographer has returned to Armenia, the land of his birth and discovers that he is a stranger: "Being here has made me from somewhere else." He also finds that he is a stranger to himself in a land he doesn't know anymore. These are the problems that Caterina Edwards explores in her fiction, drama, and essays. This central question of identity, "Who am I?" and its many ramifications as a woman, as an immigrant, as a Canadian on the prairies and as a writer are the subjects of her first novel, *The Lion's Mouth*, and of her early stories. Is this sense of identity linked to a physical environment? Edwards' fascination with this question has its roots in her own life experiences as an immigrant girl, as the daughter of an Italian mother and English father, as a person born in England but raised in Alberta. Edwards spent many summers back in Venice, Italy, with relatives. The return journey of self-discovery is an important motif in *The Lion's Mouth* and in several stories. After attending the University of Alberta Caterina Edwards married an American student of Sicilian origins and the couple settled in Edmonton to raise a family. From this point of view she has been able to explore the relationships between northern and southern Italy. It is a life full of contrasts and rich possibilities, amply exploited in her diverse literary works.

When the young Caterina Edwards began writing about the Italian immigrant experience in the 1970s there were no models for her in Canadian literature. She was the first Italian-Canadian woman writer in western Canada and, in 1982, *The Lion's Mouth* was the first Canadian novel to combine ethnicity with feminist questions. In 1986 *Terra straniera* was the first play about Italian immigrants to be staged in the prairies. It was later published as *Homeground* (1990). As a woman writer marginalised in the prairies she had the freedom to experiment with different forms and to produce work in a variety of genres: short stories, novellas, novels, a play, and essays.

Living far away from Toronto, the centre of Canadian publishing, means that you publish with small presses, that your books only get reviewed in regional papers, if at all, and that distribution and sales of your books are dependent on anomalies of chance. It also means that you are away from the hype of the centres of power and are able to focus on your art. You can treat unpopular subjects, you can explore new perspectives, you can write the way you want.

Bianca, the main character in *The Lion's Mouth*, seems to be compelled to write, and readers cannot help but see in this a reflection of the author's own need to tell the stories of new arrivals to Canada and of their links to the old country. The work of many ethnic minority writers has this transparent link to the lived experience, and the shared understanding with the minority reader that the writer is also giving voice to the silent ethnic community. Thus the necessity to tell the story is not only a personal drive for artistic expression but a public role the writer-storyteller must fulfill in the larger society. These are roles which Caterina Edwards recognizes very well and which she articulates in several of her works and in her essays, such as "A Playwright's Experience."

There is also a dark side to the examined life. In her essay, "Sublimation and Satisfaction," Edwards explores the autobiographical impulse and how it has been perverted in modern popular culture into exercises in exhibitionism and voyeurism. In contrast to this self-deception she expresses the honest quest for self-discovery:

> We construct a self from the multiplicity of selves that we live. We make sense of ourselves in the process of creating our story. And paradoxically this self-filled project connects us to others. By making the private public the writer is less alone. We speak to a community and as part of a community (323).

At various times and for many years Caterina Edwards has been a teacher of English and creative writing at institutions in Edmonton: Grant MacEwan Community College, the University of Alberta and Athabasca University. This work combines two of her major interests: her own writing and encouraging other writers. It also combines two aspects of her being: the private act of writing with the public role of teacher and mentor. These are often difficult roles to combine. The many Canadian writers who have also been teachers can testify to the conflict, the different demands and the lack of time. Add to this the fact that Edwards is also a wife and mother, and we can appreciate the pressures at work. Similar conflicts are sometimes reflected in her characters. In *A Whiter Shade of Pale* George is a provincial government lawyer who would rather be an archeologist studying the Etruscans. Marco in *The Lion's Mouth* is an architect who seems more inclined to be an artist or political activist. Both men have the added preoccupations of difficult family situations.

The life and work of most writers is more complicated than a schematic dichotomy between private desire and public demands; nevertheless, it is sometimes easier to understand the writer and the work if we look at the many forces at work on an individual. What is the relationship between life writing and fiction? Is creative writing only a private act or does it have a social role to play in society? Is writing in a realistic manner passé? These are some of the questions which Edwards tries to deal with in her dialogues with other writers like Jacqueline Dumas. On panels during meetings of the Writers' Guild of Alberta and the Association of Italian-Canadian Writers she can be trusted to articulate her views on these issues. In her many public statements about the state of letters she demonstrates a profound sense of the craft of writing, a sense which she is able to impart to her students as an inspired teacher.

Edwards was raised in a home where they spoke both English and Italian. This gives her a perspective on the English language often found among Italian-Canadian writers, but not among unilingual English authors. What is the origin and meaning of some of our English words and what are their connections to other languages? How do you translate from one language into another and from one culture into another? How do you use foreign words in your English writing in Canada? What is the role of French and of Italian?

Caterina Edwards is married to Marco LoVerso, so her legal name is Caterina LoVerso. The fact that she writes under her maiden name, Edwards, is an indication of her concern with personal identity and the shifts it can take in life. There is an ironic anecdote about this shift and possible loss of name and identity. In writing about Bianca, the main character in *The Lion's Mouth,* I called her Bianca Bolcato, giving her the same last name as her Italian cousin in the novel, Marco Bolcato. A couple of other male critics perpetuated this careless error. It took a woman critic, Licia Canton, to point out that Bianca's last name is Mazzin, not Bolcato. It took a woman to notice this discrepancy, a woman from Quebec where, since 1981, married women have been legally required to keep their maiden names. In the novel Marco acts as Bianca's alter ego and so the name shift has symbolic as well as psychological ramifications.

Personal identity in all aspects is one of the most important themes in Edwards' writing. From my perspective, and from my early experience in Canada as an immigrant, I see this preoccupation with identity as a normal outgrowth of the dislocation, of the translation of first names, of the difficulty with new languages, of the translation of daily reality, of the need to keep links with the old culture and country. In *Homeground* Maria tries to maintain this link with Italy through rituals, the ritual of water and salt, but also the family rituals of telling stories and singing Italian songs around the kitchen table. This is also a motif in her short stories, "The Last Young Man" and "Prima Vera."

Part of Edwards' preoccupation with personal identity is her attention to history, both family stories and social history. In the essay, "Where the Heart Is," she talks about her own family history in Venice and Wales. For her Canadian characters the history of Europe is not a series of remote events, but actions which are directly linked to their personal lives. Bianca, by way of Marco, revisits a Venice of high culture and pervasive corruption. A history which Marco cannot escape and which even effects Bianca in Edmonton. In the novella, *Becoming Emma,* Aida is haunted by events in the recent history of Latvia. In *A Whiter Shade of Pale* George is living another life as an archeologist in Italy excavating Etruscan ruins. World War II is in the background of Maria and Cesare in *Homeground* as they are forced to emigrate because of postwar poverty. They later find they cannot return to Italy and resume their lives there; instead they move back to Canada.

In addition to being conscious of history, Edwards makes us aware of place. It is ironic that this author who has written so much about Italy is very much a regional writer of the prairies. This strong sense of place is evident in all her works and she has often wondered out loud if this regionalism has not limited her appeal in the rest of Canada. A regional identity is a two-edged sword, and for Edwards this has been the case. Like many other regional authors Edwards writes in the realist tradition. The scale of the Alberta prairies and mountains is so great that there seems little need for fantastic fictions. The history of immigrants and settlers while epic in scale is often depicted in everyday prose.

Many of Edwards' characters want to become part of the new society. In *Becoming Emma,* Aida, the displaced Latvian girl, becomes a naturalized American and changes her name to Emma. "It was the next step in the process by which they were being transformed from free floating specks, blown here and there, at the mercy of the winds of chance, into something settled, rooted, a natural part of the landscape"(82).

The identity of characters in Edwards' narratives are always bound up with a sense of place. It is a concrete place with a physical geography and a climate. We cannot escape climate in Canada, and certainly in Alberta it is ever-present. It is a climate of distinct seasons which makes us constantly aware of place, our body's relationship to the outdoors. The harsh climate of the Canadian winter means that you cannot take this relationship for granted. Many of the Italian characters complain about this climate. They are aware that the winter can kill you and that the many Canadian stories of death in the snow are not hyperbole but reflections of reality. *Homeground* begins with reference to a friend, Gigietto Moro, who died in Whitehorse, Yukon.

One prairie writer dismissed these Italian immigrant characters as people who are "whoring after palm trees." It is a remark which demonstrates ignorance of Italian immigration to Canada. The 800 Italians who went to Yellowknife in the 1950s and 1960s to work in the mines is an indication that they were not afraid of the north. An Alberta pioneer, Giorgio Pocaterra homesteaded a ranch in Kananaskis in 1909. Frank Paci's early novels are set in Sault Ste. Marie and Lake Superior. Peter Oliva's first novel, *Drowning in Darkness,* is set in the Crowsnest Pass area where many Italians worked in the coal mines. My grandfather who worked in Mattawa, in Northern Ontario in 1906, was not afraid of the Canadian bush. It is this background of sacrifice and toil in any location which is reflected in the fiction of Italian-Canadian writers.

Much of Edwards' fiction demonstrates a profound sense of community. She is speaking for a minority community in western Canada which has been voiceless. In this recognition of her social role as a writer in the community she has much in common with other ethnic minority writers in the prairies, like Myrna Kostash, and with aboriginal writers. We get a sense of this community voice in many of her short stories which retell the peculiar experiences of immigrants. In many ways these are shared stories which emerge from the community. In her personal essay, "Care Calling Care," Edwards relates her experience in caring for her dying father-in-law, Manuele. In telling us how she and her husband worked month after month in meeting the physical and emotional needs of a paralyzed man she demonstrates this sense of community and the lessons she learned:

> When Manuele called me a princess in a tower, he wasn't entirely wrong. My tower was built from books and stories and ideas. None were wrong or false. But I have still fallen out, fallen to earth – grounded by the weight of my experience (216).

The realism in her prose is reminiscent of other prairie artists who honestly try to capture a world seen for the first time. I am reminded of the Saskatchewan painter, Alan Sap, who simply records and interprets the everyday life of his community.

The sense of community is most evident in the play, *Homeground*, where the characters not only share meals and songs around the table but also try to care for one another. This sense of social responsibility is an important part of the conflict in this play. The characters debate where they belong; where their true home is. They all feel that it is back in Italy, and they return there near the end of the play, only to find that in Italy relatives let Lucio kill himself. The people in Italy apparently were less socially responsible than those in Canada who saved Lucio from harming himself.

In her essay, "The Playwright's Experience," Edwards explains the public participation in the production of her play, *Terra straniera*, and the continuing community reaction to the performances. She discovered that there was an immigrant community wanting to be heard and that she was playing a vital role in giving them a voice. "I could not write a novel or a story that would be accessible to them. Their English was just not good enough. But the play – that spoke to them" (108).

In the summer of 1986, *Terra straniera* was a major hit when it premiered at the Edmonton Fringe Festival. Here was the first play that examined the experience of Italian immigrants in Western Canada. How do you depict such an experience and avoid negative stereotypes? One of the ways Edwards did this was to have all the characters speak in articulate English rather that in broken English or Italian accents. This controversy over the language carried on for weeks and it continued when the play was published. The Italian title of the play was questioned. Do we keep the original Italian title, a reference from an old immigrant folk song, or do we use a more accessible English title? When it went to press the play's title was changed from *Terra straniera* (Strange Land) to a term which had the opposite meaning, *Homeground*. The meanings are in keeping with the different perspectives from the two languages. For an Italian immigrant Canada is a strange land; but for an English-speaking resident it can be home. This is an example when direct translation would not have brought out these different points of view.

In her many published essays and in her talks Edwards often addresses the role of the writer in general and that of a woman writer in the prairies. In her article, "From Sea to C Minus," she argues against a blind adherence to the latest theory at the cost of free creative expression. "The practitioners of new theories (deconstruction, some types of feminist theory, cultural materialism, postcolonial studies and so on) have also had an inhibiting and divisive effect on Canadian writing . . . " She is conscious of the many pressures operating on a modern writer: the need for artistic integrity as opposed to financial success; the need for broad reader reception as opposed to only academic recognition; the need for freedom of expression as opposed to simple excess. All of these conflicts are evident in Edwards' writing career. And in the relative isolation of Edmonton, Alberta, they become more pronounced.

Probably more so than other Italian-Canadian writers, and maybe because her name does not end in a vowel, Caterina Edwards has consciously searched for the meaning of being a writer with two identities. The search begins in *The Lion's Mouth* and it continues into the play and the novellas. It is the question that haunts essay after essay.

In the pristine air of Edmonton such questions can be seen more clearly, but they cannot be answered any more easily than they can in the multicultural crowding of Toronto.

We have more space in the prairies, but do we have more choices?

In Egoyan's film, *Calendar*, the wife decides to stay in Armenia rather than return to Canada with her photographer husband. Is this a way of returning home to the homeland? Do we only feel a sense of belonging in the land were we are born? It is a choice which haunts many of the characters in Edwards' stories; it is a choice which tempts many immigrants. In one of her first short stories, "Island of the Nightingales," Edwards explored this dilemma. In preparing a new collection of her stories she had the opportunity to revise this early story which takes place on the Island of Lussino in the Adriatic, an island which is now part of Croatia. Because of the recent wars in the Balkans western readers know much more about the ethnic divisions in the region than they did in 1980 when the story first appeared. Edwards is now able to integrate some of this knowledge into the story. She can now use some of the strange names, Velilosinj, Rovenska, Malilosinj, Svet Petar, and Rijeka. She is able to explore the meaning of these names: Lussingrande (Italian) or Lussino and Velilosinj (Croatian):

> Some say that the name Lussino came from *usignuolo*, the nightingale . . . I read that some thought that the name Lussino came from *lusinga*, to enchant . . . but also to delude, to flatter, to deceive, from the German word *lausinga*, a lie.

In seeking artistic truth the writer must also confront the lie. In the end Caterina Edwards is a creative writer, an artist, whose work stands on its own and will be judged for its intrinsic and social value.

Entrapped Women
Edwards' Short Stories

ELIZABETH SARLO-HAYES

In 1985 Dino Minni argued that the short story, at its best, always deals with outside figures, marginal people. Immigrants fall easily into this category and so the short story in Canada can be read as an ethnic genre. The first example that Minni gives to support his thesis is Caterina Edwards' 1973 story, "The Last Young Man." I begin with this controversial essay because my own work on Edwards' short stories elaborates aspects of this thesis in terms of the condition and depiction of women in Italian-Canadian writing.

Now Minni's thesis is built on the arguments of Frank O'Connor about the nature of the short story form in European literature (1965). An accomplished short story writer himself, O'Connor, identified some important characteristics common to this genre: the protagonist is usually an outsider, a little person; the narrative revolves around one major incident; there is an awareness of human loneliness; the normal order of society is disrupted; there is often a mixture of elements such as humor and tragedy, irony and naivete, and these stories often being *in medias res*. I repeat these characteristics here because they all apply to the short stories of Caterina Edwards, which is to say that she is a Canadian writer who is carrying on in the great narrative tradition of European literature. And I cannot help reading into her work the influence of Italian stories, both from the folklore of the *contadini* and the published tales of Moravia, Pirandello, and Verga. All of these influences have been transformed by Edwards through her experiences as a woman writer in the prairies and as an immigrant. Her depiction of immigrant women is a major contribution to Canadian literature. What makes Edwards' stories particularly rich is that, beyond the sociological links with the history of immigration, they are "poetic in their focus" on women's internal conditions and feelings. Through their "metaphoric patterns" these stories give us a glimpse of life at a fundamental psychological level (Metcalf, 175). These brief, dense stories radiate out to many common subjects.

Beyond the relatively common subjects of alienation, cultural resistance, and nostalgia for the homeland, the theme of female entrapment is pervasive among the writers of Italian-Canadian immigrant fiction. This preoccupation has likely evolved from a variety of factors including women's frequent lack of voice in the emigration process, the coercive marital circumstances of many, and the women's comparative lack of contact with the outside world.

In his 1994 work, *Echo,* Joseph Pivato discussed the theme of entrapment: "This image of the body restricted or imprisoned in some way is one that haunts the writing of Italian-Canadian women" (162). Referring to Nora Moratti, the protagonist of Maria Ardizzi's *Made in Italy*, he states that Nora "sees her whole life . . . as an existence in a narrow cage and she . . . ends her days trapped in a wheelchair, helpless and hopeless" (188). Pivato goes on to explain that other women writers have also used forms of physical handicap or restriction as metaphors to explore the condition of immigrant women.

It is worth noting that while historical or factual accounts only offer the qualified assertion that women were denied a "formal voice" (Iacovetta, 83) in the emigration process, fictional writings such as those discussed here strongly suggest that women had no voice.

> In my town there was no room for those who didn't conform to the ways of tradition . . . The women had no choices; the judgement of the elders accompanied them from birth and if along the way they happened to err, the unfavorable judgement remained attached to them for life, like a jail sentence (Ardizzi, 23).

These are the words of Ardizzi's Nora who admits to having naively bought into the immigrant myth of a better life with more freedom and opportunities, yet who also recognizes the powerlessness of most immigrant women and that she, like many others, is caught in a prison of social and cultural isolation.

In *Mating in Captivity* Genni Gunn not only conveys the bondage implied by her book's title, she also demonstrates her belief that when first-generation immigrant women relocated to Canada, "most did not do so out of choice, but because it was expected of them as wives and daughters" (60). By employing phrases such as "he lassoed his family," and "mother, wife, daughters, women with no power" (63), Gunn illustrates the vulnerability and powerlessness of many Italian immigrant women.

Similarly, in a personal interview Gianna Patriarca reveals, through references to her mother's tears, sadness, and inability to laugh, that the decision to emigrate was not her mother's. "It was a world without choices and people said you had to be with your husband" (1995).

The Marias

It becomes apparent that regardless of what the sociological facts suggest, the theme of entrapment prevails among the writers of Italian-Canadian fiction. Caterina Edwards demonstrates how the traumatic process of emigration trapped many women. In looking first at what I refer to as her three Maria works, we see how in each case leaving Italy is not voluntary. Edwards' women protest, resist and literally beg not to be sent away, but their pleas are in vain. Nowhere is this better illustrated than in "The Last Young Man." In this story the young bride, Maria, scarcely knows her husband and desperately does not want to leave Italy. However, her father forces her to go telling her: "You are no longer a child. You must follow your husband" (25). Maria cries and protests that she cannot go, that Canada is too far away. She asks her father how he can do this to her. Yet with a sense of futility and betrayal, Maria soon realizes that her words will not make any difference in her father's determination. "He was deserting her because he was afraid of the gossip if she didn't join her husband. He cared more for the opinion of the village than for her" (25).

Even Maria's marriage, when viewed retrospectively, appears to be a trap – a whirlwind affair in which she finds herself overwhelmed and "mesmerized" by her prospective husband's enthusiasm and intensity rather than fully cognizant of the repercussions of this major event. Then, all at once, there she is, dressed in her cousin's "tight wedding dress" with Beppi "putting a ring on her hand" (26). Instead of being perceived as symbols of beauty and love, Edwards has, through her description, effectively reduced both the wedding dress and the ring to bondage motifs. Moreover, even her father's promise that she can return to Italy, but only if she finds Canada intolerable which he is certain will not be the case, leaves Maria realizing that she is indeed trapped. She is left knowing that for her, like a fly enmeshed in a spider's web, "there is no way out" (26).

In this short story we also see a clear example of the genre as outlined by Frank O'Connor: the powerless protagonist, a lonely person in a society were the normal order has been disrupted by one major event, in this case her emigration. We are in the middle of a story which seems to have no end.

Edwards' "Prima Vera" bears a number of similarities to "The Last Young Man." Maria's emigration, although related in less detail, has identical elements, though the name of the husband is different. This aspect in itself merits consideration if only to speculate whether Edwards is making Maria representative of a number of women who found themselves caught in similarly unenviable situations. In "Prima Vera" Maria also "finds" herself in her cousin's wedding dress repeating the "hallowed" wedding vows. There is no mistaking the satirical edge to Edwards' phrasing here. Nor is there any way to see Maria except as she sees herself – as a victim. She is a victim who finds herself able to think only after she is "released from the force" (132) of her husband's choice.

Throughout this short story, Maria's reflection on her marriage, "So far. And to a man I don't know" (130) echoes and evolves into a refrain highlighting not only her status as male property, but her inescapable fate.

In Edwards' play, *Homeground,* Maria is a little older. She seems to be the Maria of "Prima Vera" five years later. At this point in her life she seems less angry and openly dissatisfied, particularly when seen in contrast to the endlessly complaining Candida. Yet much of her apparent adjustment can be more accurately seen as resignation. Maria's willingness to dwell on negativity, her wishful lullabies and her frequent reluctance to focus on reality all seem to indicate an abdication of her role as the voice of female immigrant angst. Additionally, when Candida tells Maria that she cannot endure another Canadian winter, Maria reveals that prior to her arrival in Canada she already knew what it was like to be an immigrant and to live among strangers in a cold city: "I knew. Winter comes. It cannot be stopped" (28). Maria's dispassionate pragmatism here is in such startling contrast to her emotional outbursts in "Prima Vera" that it is frightening. It is as though she is only a shell of her former self, saying and doing what she thinks she should be saying and doing, but not truly alive. She no longer even leaves her house. She is like an animal who has been tied up for so long it no longer knows how to be free.

As well as being a metaphor for their sense of alienation, the physical environment of Canada, and more specifically the prairies, creates feelings of entrapment for Edwards' immigrant women. Ironically, instead of instilling them with a sense of breathing room and freedom, the huge open fields and comparatively cold climate have the opposite effect. It is as though once they are ensconced in their "flimsy" little houses these women become agoraphobic. In all three situations, each of the women verbalize their intense dislike of the Canadian climate and the prairie landscape, and exhibit behaviour which demonstrates an avoidance of both. In "Prima Vera" Maria feels as thought she is "a prisoner of this cold country" and says that her very thoughts are "freezing into the shape of the rooms and the furniture" (128). But it is not only the cold which traps her. It is the featurelessness of the relentlessly white and frozen prairie landscape. In this icy absence she is without a reference point, she is without something, *anything* to which she can relate. It is little wonder, then, that she stays inside her house, which despite its flimsiness, is at least tangible.

In "The Last Young Man" Maria also employs the language of bondage as she talks about being "locked" in her house for months at a time. Again mention is made of her thoughts "freezing into the shape of the rooms" (27). Because she cannot get herself mentally beyond the snow and cold, her thoughts and imagination stagnate until she becomes a prisoner of her own mind. While she talks about venturing out into the cold "a submission to a physical assault"(28), rather than surrendering to its malevolence, she remains its prisoner. Even in her dreams Maria cannot seem to escape stagnation and futility – she just keeps on dreaming the same frustrating dream over and over again.

In *Homeground* although Maria is more resigned to life in Canada than her counterparts, she avoids leaving her house and is trapped into an endless cycle of housework, cooking, and childcare. Even when she is encouraged and given the opportunity to get out, Maria does not budge. Despite the passage of time, she is afraid in this new world, afraid *of* this new world. She relies instead on old wives' tales and on rituals believing that only in these old ways, "oil and salt, flame and water" (78), is there any safety for herself or her children. Interestingly, she also uses the language of bondage when speaking to her child. She regretfully says, "I should have had you swaddled after you were born" (78).

Beyond the intimidating physicality of Canada and the agoraphobic state it induces in these women, there is also a claustrophobic feeling to which all three Marias give voice. This is not at all the contradiction it initially appears to be, nor is it particularly surprising. In Italy these women had been used to living *outside*. Consequently, when faced with the necessity and inevitability of living completely *inside* for at least half of the year, there is a natural resistance to being "holed up" like a hibernating animal. Because of the protagonist's compounding pregnancy, this sense of claustrophobic entrapment is probably best expressed in "Prima Vera." Maria has grown huge in this first pregnancy and her enormous weight gain has resulted in other health risks. Her condition further confines her. She is forced to lie on her back, "forced to lie as if already laid out" (128). Her painfully swollen feet can barely move and she thinks longingly of the way her feet used to run freely back in Italy. Now it is only her heart that is "runaway." She is "stuck to this miserable house," with its "fragile walls trying to hold off snow, trying to keep back the cold" (129), walls that she can feel being steadily weakened. In this instance (and in all three stories at some point) Maria can be seen metaphorically as being the house. She is the fragile structure being steadily weakened in this harsh alien environment.

In "The Last Young Man" when Maria feels so alone after Luigino leaves for Italy, she refers to the silent, empty house that fills her with fear. Her last boarder closes the door behind him and she feels simultaneously abandoned and confined. Both the door and the house serve as motifs of confinement and the house itself, as in "Prima Vera," is symbolic of her vacant yet precarious emotional state. She too is afraid of being exposed. She too realizes that her house both protects and entraps her. Neither of the two Marias is ready or willing to let go of that flimsy structure, that piece of themselves that will not be let down because it refuses to trust. Even the Maria in *Homeground*, who appears more accepting than the others, has tremendous difficulty trusting and, therefore, remains, like the other Marias, a prisoner in her own house.

Aside from feeling trapped by the coercive circumstances of their emigration and the cold Canadian climate, Italian immigrant women have been most confined by what Maria Ardizzi calls the *"gabbia stretta,"* the narrow cage from the inability to communicate in the majority language. Because they often remained in the private sphere of domestic life and because they usually did not have access to the language training programs available to their spouses, Italian immigrant women frequently did not learn English. The inability to communicate with the outside world left these women further stymied and silenced.

Looking first at the pregnant Maria, it becomes clear that her ignorance of English has implications for her health and that of her baby. Maria fails to comprehend what her obstetrician tells her about her own precarious health. He uses the terms "toxemia" and "preeclampsia" but she does not know what these words or even simpler words mean. Nor does she realize the inherent risks involved in not knowing the language of the dominant culture. Compounding this communication gap is the medical community's contemptuous attitude. In their eyes she is just another backward "disgusting Italian" (140), who eats too much spaghetti. Admittedly, this assessment is unfair as well as blatantly racist but as long as Maria remains ignorant of the English language she is trapped in these stereotypes of Italians.

In "The Last Young Man" Maria's inability to speak English renders her unable to communicate with and relate to her own children. While her children have adopted the language of *their* country, she remains mired down because she speaks only Italian. Her deficiency becomes glaringly apparent to her once her last Italian boarder leaves and she realizes that unless she learns English she will have no one with whom she can communicate. As it is, her older children have already grown away from her and even her baby, Lella, mocks her speech and call her "funny mummy" (27). Despite her overt dissimilarity to her mother, Lella can be seen as Maria's alter ego. However, Lella's disobedient, strong-willed nature suggests that it is highly unlikely that *she* will ever be trapped into a life she does not want to live. And as Maria watches her daughter run out the door she recognizes that, as surely as Lella is growing and becoming, she is stagnating. She recognizes that it was her obedience that trapped her here in the first place. She sees in Lella all the opportunities she might have had – opportunities for personal growth and freedom. Simultaneously though, it may also be seen, by the way in which she physically unites herself with Lella in the final scene, that Maria realizes that only through effort and adjustment will she both free herself and be enabled to truly communicate with and love her children.

In *Homeground* we see that despite her apparent resignation to life in Canada, Maria's failure to learn English results in an almost palpable fear of the outside world. She attempts to ignore her phone but when that is made impossible she becomes upset and depressed because she cannot understand anything. She says she hates the phone, but what she actually hates is that her ignorance of English makes her feel more alienated and thus more trapped within herself. Later in the play, Maria is visibly shaken by the sudden realization that her son, her only bond to Canada, has been thoroughly North Americanized. However, she cannot articulate her emotions. Consequently, in her frustration and grief she leaves the room crying: "Without the words, I cannot . . . Cannot . . . I. Forgive me" (64). At this point, Maria fully understands that which she has only partially understood before – that without the language she is paralyzed. Like Ardizzi's Nora, she is thoroughly silenced and trapped.

Returning Home

Reviewing the three Maria stories it appears as though all of these women's unhappiness and feelings of entrapment stem from their emigration from a familiar Italy to Canada. If this is so, does the solution to their woes, to their lack of freedom lie in a return to Italy? Will returning set them free? In a discussion of this topic Joseph Pivato observes that recent social history indicates that an increasing number of Italian immigrants are returning to their home towns. He adds that "for some people the return to Italy is an attempt to return to the past. Many have idealized the innocence and simplicity of their village life before emigration and forgotten the poverty, the absent fathers and the broken families"(1994, 191). Furthermore, as Dino Minni has explained, once emigration has occurred, it is virtually impossible to revert to that pre-emigrant state and not see Italy through Canadian eyes (1985, 73). This is certainly the case with Maria's family in *Homeground*. They move back to Italy only to find in the end that they no longer belong there.

This phenomenon re-appears in four other stories by Edwards: "Island of the Nightingales," "On a Platter," "Everlasting Life," and "Home and Away." More importantly, these works not only demonstrate the impossibility of returning to the pre-emigrant mind set, but the sense of entrapment which recognizes no geographical boundaries and which has captured Edwards' literary imagination as thoroughly as it has captured her characters' souls. To paraphrase John Metcalf, these stories in their metaphoric texture move imagistically as poems do.

In the "Island of the Nightingales," the totally Canadianized Angela visits Italy during her summer break from college. Angela is part of the "free-love" 1960s generation but is trapped by her inability to commit herself to anyone or anything. She feels physically free in wandering the Italian countryside, yet, at the same time, she feels imprisoned by the country's rigid social/sexual mores. Conversely in Canada, despite its confining climate which "distances her from the earth" (187), she feels sexually free and so she simultaneously juggles her two lovers. Images, motifs, and the language of entrapment abound throughout "Island of the Nightingales." At the beginning of this story Angela has a frightening experience involving a group of Frenchmen surrounding her in a seductive dance: "They had formed a circle ... I tried going forward again, but they moved with me, a tight imprisoning circle of Europeans" (183). Shortly afterwards, she sees a woman who captures her attention, a woman whose lover's hand "encircles her wrists" (184). This is a person to whom she can immediately relate because of the "manacling" actions of the man at her side, because of this "struggle for possession through containment" (184).

At the same time, Angela admires this beautiful woman for her seeming ability to successfully balance the two men in her life. She would like to be able to exert this control herself instead of being forever tied to the unspoken "rules of the relationship" (188). She would like to break free but she does not know how. She realizes that she is being pushed at by both sides, by both Tony and Darryl (her Italian and Canadian identities perhaps?). Her only escape seems to be in a drug-induced withdrawal. Consequently, when Angela meets her doppelgänger, she becomes obsessed with discovering her secret – how can this woman be so free, especially in a country still so bound to sexual double standards?

It is not long, however, before Angela discovers that this woman is trapped into a "walled cycle" (193). Yet, because she has erroneously equated promiscuity and indecision with freedom, Angela continuously vacillates between the two men (Tony and Darryl) and two countries (Italy and Canada) in her life. What she gradually comes to see is that her vacillation creates so much stress and takes up so much of her time and energy, that she is the proverbial mouse caught in the maze. Moreover, until she lets go of the people and the rules which run her life, she can run but she will not get anywhere and she will never be free.

This short story is a fine example of the genre as described by Minni and O'Connor: the narrator is a powerless outsider who undergoes a self-discovery through the experience of one incident. The normal order of things is disrupted as she finds herself on the island of Lussino in the Adriatic in a society at once restricting and chaotic. While she is visiting her Italian aunts she is not really in Italy but on a Croatian island which was officially part of Yugoslavia. The juxtaposition of society in Canada with her Italian trip makes Angela re-evaluate her life choices.

In Edwards' "On A Platter" the central female character, Fulvia, is also powerless and trapped. Rather than day-to-day realities, as in the case of Angela, Fulvia is trapped by memories. She has a thriving business in Edmonton, friends, money, and a husband and daughter who love her, yet, despite these outward manifestations of success and personal freedom, Fulvia remains "caught and locked in memory" (344). She sees Italy and her early life there as the source of her unhappiness and consequently attempts to banish both from her mind. Her childhood is described as "closed off" and "walled up, thousands of miles and twenty years away" (344). But it is Fulvia herself who is closed off and walled up for even if she wanted to call up her memories and speak of them, she believes that what lurks "behind those stone walls topped with broken glass" (345), cannot be voiced. Even the nature of Fulvia's memories tends to be beyond her control. Rather than scenes, she recalls sensations, sensations of darkness, enclosure, and shame all of which she associates with her childhood and, more importantly, with Italy. Here too it should be noted that Edwards employs the language of confinement and bondage to effectively convey Fulvia's sense of entrapment. Similarly, when Fulvia herself thinks back to her wedding day, she also uses this language to draw a contrast between Canada and Italy, and to reassure herself that she made her vow "here in a clean, bare Canadian church, not over there encased in the baroque excess of St. Agatha's" (346). Fulvia has nightmares involving this church and all its riotous confusion. These nightmares threaten to smother her "like a white-gauze curtain" (348).

Fulvia struggles to break free of her smothering memories yet when she reminds herself that there is no undoing the past, no going back, she feels powerless. This sense of powerlessness arises not only out of her inability to get rid of her negative memories but, as well, her inability to access those that are positive. Indeed, she is as trapped in Canada with its cold, clean air as she was amid all the heat and excessiveness of Italy. At this critical point in her life (when her own health hangs in the balance) she can neither move forward nor backward. Her longtime friend, Anne, observes that Fulvia trusts no one. And although she dismisses Anne's opinion, Fulvia recognizes that until she can open her "inner door" along with her "iced over one" (350), until she can once again allow someone to touch her, she will remain as trapped and cut off from herself as the sacrificial "virgin breasts" on the platter.

The baroque image of breasts on a platter is a metaphor for physical and psychological mutilation, and graphically captures the oppressive sense of self-sacrifice which the story tries to attack. Parallel to this ritual of martyrdom is the one for death in an early Edwards story, "Everlasting Life." Here again duty becomes a trap for women.

As the title, "Everlasting Life," suggests, there is a sense of entrapment involving both the Italian mother, Augusta, and her immigrant daughter, Aurora. Both are trapped in their respective roles, and both in their own ways struggle to break free of their lives and backgrounds. For the thoroughly Canadianized Aurora, the struggle is made easier if only from the perspective of her comparative youth. As a young woman, Aurora was severely repressed and it was only once she came to Canada that she began to discover a climate of freedom and opportunity which did not exist in Italy. Now that she is back in Italy caring for her ailing mother, Aurora again feels that former sense of confinement. Young girls may be wearing jeans but the sexual double standard remains intact. Women are still trapped and restricted by public opinion and expectation. Nothing has really changed.

This environment of confined stagnation terrifies Aurora who has nightmares of being trapped in some kind of Thesean cycle of futility. Additionally, Aurora is trapped by her own strong sense of filial obligation, an obligation which she refuses to pass on to her own children. This obligation imprisons her in this small, hot, enveloping room, imprisons her with these old women who are perpetually dressed in black. These vultures who wait for death and who thrive on its momentousness and spectacle.

Ironically, of those who are waiting for death no one is more anxious that Augusta herself. She is well aware of her daughter's views regarding filial obligation and is consequently equally well aware that Aurora has no desire to be with her at this time. She does not ask for the Kevorkian-like assistance that Signora Margherita does, but her silence and in her sadness Augusta demonstrates that she has given up, that there is no more fight in her. Nevertheless, life continues to entrap her. We see evidence of this corporal entrapment most clearly in Edwards' description of her physical appearance. Although Augusta's hair is still dark and thick, she no longer walks and her flesh is a hanging shapeless mess – as spiritless as her soul. The mother that Aurora once knew has "survived only in remnants" (89). Meanwhile, her enormous black eyes have become "like two screens," screens which reflect the outside but reveal nothing from within. As surely as she has been trapped all these years by societal expectations of her, Augusta is now trapped within herself. She is buried somewhere beneath her heavy purple flesh, somewhere behind those enormous reflecting eyes. When Augusta asks her daughter to "pull her up" (89), the words are both a literal and metaphorical call for help. She will not actually utter the words "help me" because she is too proud and too aware of Aurora's reluctance.

Gradually Aurora becomes aware that the death-focused environment that her mother has been forced to inhabit is both emotionally and psychologically unhealthy. Italy may have a stranglehold on its women, but they in turn have a stranglehold on Augusta. Aurora also sees in Augusta the potential for her own old age. She has told her children they owe her nothing, so who, then, will look out for her? Rather abruptly, Aurora decides to take her mother back to Canada with her. Her decision signifies not only the authenticity of Aurora's feelings toward her mother, but a change in her life view. Obligation may have sent her back to Italy, but it is love and loyalty that move her to bring her mother with her to Canada. Once Aurora sees the fleeting fear, and the even more fleeting amusement, once she sees the life still beating within her, she realizes that her mother is being buried alive. Aurora cannot turn away from her own mother; she cannot abandon her to these parasites just waiting to seize upon her death as their next moment of celebration. She must take the necessary risks in order to give her mother some quality to the life she has left. "Everlasting life" is not a blessing, but a curse. It is a jail sentence which Aurora comes to realize that she alone has the power to lift.

In "Home and Away" there is the vicarious return of the immigrant parents through their daughter who must go through the ritual of seeing the locations of her parents' nostalgia: "I visited all your old stomping grounds like I knew you'd want me to: the café in the piazza, the dance pavilion by the sea, Zio Antonio's farm, where Dad proposed, San Giovanni where you were married." The dutiful daughter writes back to her parents, but she must confess she found it stifling being "fussed over from morning to night" by her Italian relatives. After a week she had to get away and find her own space and her own Italy. She cannot live in the past, the Italy of her parents, and she must come to terms with important decisions in her own life. Is Canada to be her home or is it another trap?

In this brief reading of selected short stories by Caterina Edwards we see the ambivalence that her women characters show to both Canada and Italy. Often Canada is depicted as both a place of entrapment for the immigrant woman and her daughters and as a place with the potential for freedom and creativity. In the last three stories examined here, especially "Island of the Nightingales" Italy (Southern Europe) is depicted as the entrapping environment. Parallel to the ambivalence of the characters is the sense of simultaneous alienation and entrapment. Edwards' women seem to be caught between two worlds and belonging in neither one nor the other. Edwards is masterfully using the compact form of the short story to capture these mini dramas in the lives of her women. In this interpretation Canada and Italy can often be read as metaphors for the human condition. Since returning to Italy is not the solution, Edwards seems to suggest that these Canadian women must explore greater autonomy, and leave behind their anger, resentment, and fear. They need to take the steps to make their lives better. Even though these women have been disappointed in the past they need to take the risk and move forward.

> Note: A first selection of Edwards' short stories, *Island of the Nightingales*, came out with Guernica Editions in 2000 and the title story was revised and expanded. Angela's name is changed to Teresa.

WORKS CITED

Ardizzi, Maria. *Made in Italy*. Toronto: Toma Publishing, 1982. Rpt. Toronto: Guernica Editions, 1999.

Edwards, Caterina . "The Last Young Man," *Journal of Canadian Fiction*, .2, 1, 1973.

―――. "Everlasting Life," *Getting Here: An Anthology*. ed. Rudy Wiebe. Edmonton: NeWest Press, 1977.

―――. "Island of the Nightingales," *More Stories from Western Canada*. eds. Rudy Wiebe and Aritha Van Herk. Toronto: Macmillan, 1980.

―――. "Prima Vera," *Ricordi: Things Remembered*. ed. C.D. Minni. Montreal: Guernica, 1989.

―――. *Homeground*. Montreal: Guernica, 1990.

―――. "On a Platter," *Boundless Alberta*. ed. Aritha Van Herk. Edmonton: NeWest Press, 1990.

―――. "Home and Away," *Other Voices*, 5,1, 1992.

―――. "Stella's Night," *Pillar's of Lace*. ed. Marisa De Franceschi. Toronto: Guernica, 1998.

Gunn, Genni. *Mating in Captivity*. Toronto: Quarry Press, 1993.

Iacovetta, Franca. *Such a Hardworking People*. Montreal: McGill-Queen's U. Press, 1992.

Metcalf, John ed. *Making It New: Contemporary Canadian Stories*. Toronto: Methuen, 1982.

Minni, C.D. "The Short Story as an Ethnic Genre," *Contrasts*. ed. J. Pivato. Montreal: Guernica, 1985, 1991 (rpt.).

O'Connor, Frank. *The Lonely Voice: A Study of the Short Story*. New York: Meridian Books, 1965.

Patriarca, Gianna. Personal interview with author, 1995.

Pivato, Joseph. *Echo*. Toronto: Guernica, 1994.

Verduyn, Christl, ed. *Literary Pluralities*. Peterborough: Broadview Press-JCS, 1998.

Edmonton Versus Venice

The Whole Truth

PETRA FACHINGER

> "The trouble with you," one man said to me, "is that you think in English and feel in Italian."
> Mary di Michele

In Caterina Edwards' *The Lion's Mouth*, the juxtaposition of Venice and Edmonton serves as the geographical trope to express the cultural difference between the "Old World" and the "New World." The novel is structured around a number of further dichotomies: Venice is associated with art and sophisticated culture while Edmonton/Canada represents nature and empty landscape. In the words of Edwards' narrator, Edmonton, "this still-infant city" is not yet "fully imagined" (60). Yet Venice pays a high price for its cultural status. In the novel, Venice of the 1970s is also associated with decay, disease, rigorous class structure, the disintegration of the family, corrupt enterprise, industrial pollution, terrorism, and last but not least, the legacy of two World Wars. Implicitly, Canada seems relatively unaffected by these ills.

The juxtaposition of "Old World" and "New World," in which the latter is usually perceived as a redemptive space, represents a fairly common narrative technique in twentieth-century Canadian literature,[1] particularly in the writing of authors with a dual cultural heritage. *The Lion's Mouth* shares its structural reliance on the above dichotomies with novels like John Richardson's *Wacousta, or The Prophecy; A Tale of the Canadas* and Henry Kreisel's *The Betrayal*. I mention the former because of its elements of the gothic, a genre that, as I will show, Caterina Edwards also draws on in her novel, and the latter because it is an Edmonton novel that bears similarities to *The Lion's Mouth*. Like *The Lion's Mouth*, *The Betrayal*, whose action moves back and forth between Edmonton and Vienna, highlights Edmonton's youth, its "unself-consciousness" (Kreisel 2) and its potential to grow. It also describes Canada as "an unsophisticated country, incapable of producing subtle works. A country of mountains and vast spaces and Indians and the mounted police" (34). While "The Old World" is a place of decay, rigid class structure, and conflict in all three novels, it also stands for "history," something that Canada, in the minds of the three narrators/authors, seems to lack.

All three novels also conclude on a positive note with regard to the future of Canada/Edmonton. Although Richardson stops short of uniting Oucanasta and Frederick de Haldimar in marriage, both Oucanasta and her brother, the Ottawa chief, do become "educators" for the de Haldimar children. When Theodore Stappler, Austrian Jewish exile in *The Betrayal*, returns to Edmonton from "the North," which is a place of healing and fulfilment for him, the city appears as the promised land: "It's magnificent to fly into this city at night. Suddenly ... out of an immense darkness there comes a great circle of light. God, how marvelous!" (211). Bianca, the narrator of *The Lion's Mouth*, shares Stappler's optimism about Edmonton's future. As she concludes in the final chapter of the novel:

> So I begin again my life in this city, this land. City: the place where the citizen is at home. I will, with the others, make this city, imagine it fully. The possibility exists. We are not yet confined by old fantasies and old blood, all the weight of what has already been done, good and bad. In our simplicity we are unhampered, untried. The energy can run free (268).

What, in the narrator's opinion, Edmonton/the "New World" has been lacking in terms of art and sophistication is finally beginning to leave an imprint on Edmonton. Edmonton's transition from prairie town to a culturally more developed centre compensates the narrator for having to let go of her "Venetian dream."

The most redeeming feature, however, which makes Bianca's utopian vision seem "possible" is Edmonton's / Canada's position at the margin or periphery. The valorization of the margin as the privileged position makes *The Lion's Mouth* not only a very Canadian novel, as I have demonstrated above, but also a postcolonial novel. Like many other postcolonial novels, *The Lion's Mouth* uses hybridization and double-voicedness as its main decentring strategies. Hybridization, as Mikhail Bakhtin defines it, is "the mixing, within a single concrete utterance, of two or more different linguistic consciousnesses, often widely separated in time and social space" (*The Dialogic Imagination*, 429, "Glossary"). Bakhtin's definition for double-voiced discourse is "another's speech in another's language, serving to express authorial intentions but in a refracted way" (324) so that double-voiced discourse is always "internally dialogized" (324). The examples of double-voiced discourse that Bakhtin cites are "comic, ironic or parodic discourse, the refracting discourse of a narrator, refracting discourse in the language of a character and finally the discourse of a whole incorporated genre" (324). In this paper, I will argue that Edwards rewrites elements of both the *Bildungsroman* and the gothic novel in addition to "dialogizing" her text through numerous intertextual references and "carnivalizing" it through various decentering devices to probe the construction of ethnic identity.

With the story of Bianca and her Venetian cousin Marco, Edwards rewrites with a twist the type of *Bildungsroman* that Charlotte Goodman calls "the male-female double *Bildungsroman*." According to Goodman, the main structural difference between the prototypical *Bildungsroman* and the male-female double *Bildungsroman* is that the former moves in a linear fashion, that is, it describes the hero's process through life, while the latter moves in a circle. It describes the shared childhood experiences of a male and a female protagonist in an idyllic environment, followed by their separation in adolescence. While the male, like the hero of the typical male *Bildungsroman*, goes on a quest to seek his fortune and gain knowledge of the world, the female is left behind. Eventually the protagonists, as, for example, Cathy and Heathcliff in *Wuthering Heights*, Maggie and Tom in *The Mill on the Floss*, and Antonia and Jim in *My Antonia* are reunited, however, tragically or unhappily. The authors of the five novels[2] on which Goodman bases her study were all critical of society's rigid differentiation between male and female gender roles, which deprives women of education and equal opportunity. Caterina Edwards inverts the paradigm of the male-female double *Bildungsroman* by ending the "hero's" career with divorce and a nervous breakdown in the "Old World" while the "heroine" manages to "exorcise her dream of Venice" (269) in the process of telling the "hero's" story, welcoming her Venetian niece to Edmonton, and by beginning to "imagine" Edmonton more "fully."

Unlike the protagonists in the male-female double *Bildungsroman* described by Goodman, Bianca and Marco do not spend their childhood in "a prelapsarian mythic garden world" (Goodman 30), but the "heroine" lives her adult life in a place conceived in similar terms. As the narrator reassesses their relationship in the epilogue: "The spell of childhood was broken . . . You are a Venetian. How can you not feel the exhaustion, the decay of the world? My kiss – hopeful and Canadian – could never awaken you from your sleep of negativism" (270). Furthermore, the "reunion" of male and female protagonist, only takes place in Bianca's imagination: "I recreate your infancy, your childhood, trying to understand. I imagine the bombings, the operation . . . Still I cannot write it in Italian, and you do not read English. I will never touch you at all" (271). While the "reunion" in the five novels that Goodman discusses "signifies a turning away from mature adult experience and a reaffirmation of the childhood world" (30-31), the "reunion" in *The Lion's Mouth* is only redemptive for the narrator, who is finally able to let go of her childhood world through the therapeutic act of writing. Although Bianca does not physically reunite with Marco and realizes that she cannot "touch" him at all because they live in separate worlds, she will be reunited with her young Venetian niece. Living on her own, Bianca will take care of Barbara, who is sent to Canada to recover from a traumatic experience.

The narrator, who at the moment of writing is in her late twenties, left Venice at the age of eight emigrating to Edmonton with her parents for economic reasons. Bianca describes her younger self as being "split into two seemingly inimical halves, not only between the time before and after, but through all my growing years: Italy in summer, Canada in winter" (108). Her inability to feel at home in either Italian or English, alienates her from both her Italian relatives in Venice and from her peers in Edmonton. The immigrant child's dilemma of being "lost in translation" has been described in many novels and autobiographies, mainly as an obstacle to full integration into the adopted society. What makes Bianca's linguistic estrangement particularly painful, however, is not the fact that her classmates tease her about her pronunciation, but the fact that it makes communicating with Marco awkward and frustrating:

> Still, when I tried to answer you, the words on my tongue were English. I paused, I stuttered, searched for the Italian equivalents. I was smooth enough with the phrases of family and home. But theory, abstract thought, seemed necessarily English, for it was the language in which I read ... My mouth wouldn't open wide enough to let the words properly roll. The Canadian style, tight and reserved, had been coded into my body and could not be unlearned (123-24).

In migrant fiction by women, a female character's psychological adjustment to a new country is often closely associated with her experience of living on the threshold of womanhood. At sixteen, Bianca falls in love with the twenty-four-year-old Marco. Not only is Marco her "Prince Charming" who awakens her with a kiss into womanhood: "Then your lips met mine. The spell of childhood was broken. I was awakened" (270), but he also is her mentor, lecturing her on photography, painting, music, and politics. But most important to her, he teaches her how to manipulate her appearance so she can look just as sophisticated as the Venetian women.

But unlike many other migrant stories about growing up in an adopted country, *The Lion's Mouth* focuses on the adult Marco in Venice, not on Bianca as she is growing up in Edmonton. When the letter with the news of Marco's hospitalization reaches her, the narrator had not seen him in several years. In the biographical chapters of *The Lion's Mouth*, that is, the chapters in which Bianca tells Marco's story, she describes the crucial events of the three days leading to his nervous breakdown. While the narrator has adjusted to the Canadian environment to the extent that "in the deepest sense" (60) she feels at home in Edmonton, Marco's life and health have been deteriorating over the years. He is unhappily married, his little son suffers from an incurable heart disease, his own stomach problems are worsening, and he unwittingly gets involved in a brigadist murder. The public assault has a traumatic effect on his young niece Barbara, who happens to be present at the scene of the shooting. Venice has lost its charm and dignity and no longer represents for him the "safe harbour" – an illusion to which Marco has been desperately clinging. Marco's mother writes in her letter to Bianca: "And I know only that my son is not getting better. He's suspended" (11). The word "suspended" fittingly describes Marco's apathy caused by anxiety, guilt, and frustration.

The narrator explains that Marco's extreme sensitivity and inability to distance himself from his surroundings are the result of his having witnessed the bombing of Zara when he was a child. The bombing had such a traumatic, and consequently somatic effect, on him that at the age of fourteen "instead of snipping away foreskin, they'd taken most of his stomach" (27). Marco feels that having witnessed the slaughter of innocent people when he was a boy has contaminated him to such a degree that he carries the genetic flaw responsible for the hole in his son's heart:

> Only in abnormality was there individuality. The abnormality of Francesco who differed in something so minute as a chromosome. His defective son. The seed of his emptiness . . . He'd seen, oh yes, he'd seen inside. Blood, a strangely warm rain in the cold November air. The bodies split. Gashed. Hanging above him. Still fresh and hot. He knew (27-28).

Bianca decides to write Marco's story and to reveal the immediate circumstances leading to Marco's final breakdown, as he is unable to do so. In the novel's prologue, the narrator insists that she "want[s] to be the one who not only knows but illuminates the truth" (11-12). "Casting [her]self in the role of champion" (10), the narrator plans to discover "the hidden path, the hidden door, rescuing [him] from [his] fortress of self, guiding [him] back to the world" (10-11).

The above quotation with its gothic overtones is indicative of another reversal, in this case not of narrative structures, but of gender roles. While the narrator takes on the role of "champion" and comes to Marco's rescue, Marco turns into the maiden in distress. But Edwards' parody of the gothic is not restricted to the reversal of gender roles. Like Jane Austen in *Northanger Abbey*, Edwards also rewrites the prototypical characters of the traditional gothic novel.[3] Marco's bosses Adolfo and Raponi represent the gothic villains with their intention to transform the Lido into another Jesolo-style tourist attraction. Marco, who is opposed to this kind of irresponsible development motivated by greed and blind commercialism, feels powerless and utterly frustrated when his boss informs him that the company is going to go ahead with the project regardless of whether or not he will cooperate. Elena, Marco's childhood sweetheart, who is beautiful and comes from a wealthy family, is the "princess." However, "princess" has turned "villain" as Marco learns when he runs into her three days before his breakdown. Elena has joined a terrorist group and, together with her companion Piero, makes Marco a reluctant accomplice in the assassination of the chief prosecutor, who was instrumental in obtaining severe penalties for members of their group.

Although Marco feels like a "victim" and is portrayed as passive and unable to take action, stereotypically feminine characteristics, the younger Bianca in her three previous attempts to write a novel about Marco, cast him as a gothic hero. The variations that the plot of this story undergoes reflect Bianca's own emotional development and changing attitude toward her adopted country. In her first attempt, she finds herself telling a story not about Marco but about "a sensitive Italian girl," who emigrated to the prairies and consequently dies of "mental and physical decay," "destroyed by the hostile, cold land" (107). Gianni, her hero and a fellow immigrant, refuses to save her and returns to Italy to become an opera singer. This plot is obviously modelled on the prototypical male *Bildungsroman*, in which the male protagonist succeeds while the female protagonist usually dies. In the second attempt, Gianni becomes more of a gothic hero. The heroine is an "innocent" Canadian traveller, the hero a "degenerate" European who seduces and abandons her "set on the path of her destruction" (159). The older narrator retrospectively blames "Canadian puritanism" and her parents' "clinging to the Italian ways" for her penchant for gothic exaggeration at this stage of her emotional development.

The Marco of the third narrative attempt is already less of a type. The narrator is interested in the past that shaped him and explores the effects that having witnessed the bombings of Zara must have had on him. In this plot, the "Canadian girl with a Venetian background" is less innocent and less the victim, "though she was still irritatingly passive" (217). The narrator remarks: "I still wanted her destroyed and wanted the destruction to spring from a genetic deficiency, a Venetian inadequacy in the face of the harshness of the new land" (217). While in the prose of Horace Walpole and Ann Radcliffe the typical gothic site is Italy, which in the English literary tradition represented the exotic and unruly, in Edwards' version of the gothic, terror and horror lurk in the Canadian landscape. Yet, what all gothic heroines have in common, be they suffering in Italy or in Canada, is their physical and emotional displacement. Once the heroine enters the gothic world, her identity begins to collapse. This loss of identity is usually caused by an encounter with the unfamiliar and incomprehensible. Arriving in Canada, Bianca feels "stripped of family, of friends, of familiar walls and buildings, of proper landscape" (109), a despair which any traditional gothic heroine, imprisoned in an Italian castle, would have shared.

One gothic convention to express the fragmentation of the self is the creation of doubled identities so that the relationship between self and other is transformed into the relationship between opposing aspects of the self. These opposing aspects of the self are often depicted as male and female energies at war within one character. The narrative focus on Marco in the younger Bianca's attempts to tell his story as well as in the novel itself becomes meaningful when one regards Marco as Bianca's dark twin, that is, her Italian self: "For you are within me, the emblem of my inner city" (59). The male-female double *Bildungsroman* shares with the gothic novel the preoccupation with doubles and a probing into the nature of masculine and feminine identity. As Charlotte Goodman points out, "unusually close, the paired male and female protagonist in each of these novels appear to function as psychological 'doubles'" (31). Goodman argues that each character may also

> embody a separate aspect of the author's own psychic life, the female character representing the author's identification with those women who have been forced to conform to traditional female gender roles, the male character, the author's desire for learning, power, mobility, autonomy. Together the male and the female character suggest the possibility

of androgynous wholeness, a state imaginable only in a mythic prelapsarian world of nature before a patriarchal culture gained ascendancy (31).

Edwards adopts the male-female paradigm not to critique gender inequality and heterosexism, but to depict the psychic life of a migrant, emotionally torn between two countries. Metaphorically speaking, Bianca reaches a stage of "androgynous wholeness," as opposed to the fragmentation of a life "split into two seemingly inimical halves" (108), through the act of telling Marco's story, which purges her of her Italian self. The message is not that a migrant needs to abandon her ethnic heritage to stay sane in an adopted country, but that she needs to learn to live in the present and develop a more intimate relationship with the country. Jack, a Canadian boyfriend of Ukrainian ancestry, helped Bianca to take the first step in forming a more intimate relationship with her environment:

> It was Jack who taught me the names of the flowers – Indian paintbrush, Queen Anne's lace, fairy bells, who taught me to recognize the different species of mushrooms, to categorize the different types of birch. He insisted I learn how to cross-country ski. Remembering my childhood struggle to learn how to skate . . . I was convinced I couldn't do it. But Jack was not easily deterred and I found I could. Gliding through the white, tree-bordered fields, gliding through the silence, the cold air not a blow but a caress on my overheated cheeks . . . in teaching me to recognize, teaching me to name, he changed me. It was as if the emotional slide through which I had been viewing the land, the slide that coloured the country oppressive and infinitely barren, flipped up

and back to be stored; a new one that painted the land familiar and supporting clicked into place (61-63).

Just as the "Old World" immigrant needs to learn new words – for which there may be no equivalents in his or her first language – to be able to comprehend and "imagine" the new environment, immigrant writers who intend to write about the new place need to modify their tools. Susanna Moodie, for example, was unable to settle on a genre in which to write *Roughing It in the Bush*. As John Thurston observes,

> Moodie's personality is split by the institution and system of *la langue* as she carries it and *la parole* as she finds it actualized in Canada. This linguistic gap is the place where we read all of the other contradictions, including the social ones. She seeks generic and social stability through language but is confused by the dialogic force of the discourse she encounters (202).

For a writer in the "New World," and particularly one with a dual cultural heritage, forming a closer relationship with the environment may imply testing traditional paradigms for their viability and alter them if found unsuitable. As I have shown, Edwards rewrites aspects of both the *Bildungsroman* and the gothic novel in *The Lion's Mouth*. Decentring strategies and intertextuality are further techniques she uses to challenge traditional ways of knowing and perceiving as well as the construction of identities.

Marco's story comes to a climax during the Venetian carnival. On his way to the *bocca di leone*, where, in a symbolic act, he intends to denounce himself for having betrayed his wife, his son, and his city, Marco struggles through the masked carnival crowd. In *Rabelais and His World*, Bakhtin claims:

> All the symbols of the carnival idiom are filled with this pathos of change and renewal, with the sense of the gay relativity of prevailing truths and authorities. We find here a characteristic logic, the peculiar logic of the "inside out" (*à l'envers*), of the "turnabout," of a continual shifting from top to bottom, from front to rear, of numerous parodies and travesties, humiliations, profanations, comic crownings and uncrownings. A second life, a second world of folk culture is thus constructed; it is to a certain extent a parody of the extracarnival life, a "world inside out" (11).

The carnival madness ironically reflects the political and emotional turmoil both Venice and the characters in the novel are experiencing. At the same time as Marco is making his way through the crowd, the brigadist shoots the prosecutor, Barbara witnesses the assassination, and Marco's wife and son return with bad news from an out-of-town visit to a heart specialist. Marco, who blames himself for not having sought appropriate medical treatment for his son more actively and for failing to prevent his boss from pursuing his development project, is ironically forced to act by the brigadists. As their messenger he identifies himself with the words: "Now is the time of action," to which the assassin replies: "a time of terrible beauty" (203). At this verbal exchange, Marco, who can see the "terribleness" but not much of the "beauty," feels that "what was lacking" is "transformation" (203). The

Venetian carnival, reduced to tourist attraction, has lost its former power to bring about change and renewal.

Furthermore, surviving manifestations of carnivalesque inversion and subversion depend on being recognized as such by the beholder. While playing in the *palazzo* Morosini when he was a boy, Marco's attention was drawn to the small stone lion on the filigreed railing, the only one facing in rather than out: "The lion had been carved out of the same pillar that formed the corner column and could not be removed without marring the whole balcony. The unknown medieval artist had been careful to make his act of rebellion permanent" (40). In the art gallery where Marco is to deliver the message to the assassin, the two men look at Gentile Bellini's *The Miracle of the Cross* before identifying themselves to each other. Pondering the meaning of the painting, their attention focuses on Bellini's decentering device and own act of "rebellion": a black figure on the edge of the painting, peering down into the water.

From her own privileged position at the periphery, the site that has inherited the carnival spirit, the narrator/Edwards deploys a variety of intertextual references in her text. Intertextual references to Dante's *La Divina Commedia*, Shakespeare's *The Merchant of Venice*, Yeats' "Easter 1916" and the old partisan song "O partigiano, portami via," to name only the most obvious, bespeak the subversive potential of literature and the dialogic force of intertextuality. The fact that the chosen texts belong to the Italian as well as the English literary tradition also bears witness to the narrator's/Edwards' dual cultural heritage. Both the narrator and Caterina Edwards demonstrate intense awareness of their cultural and literary ethnic roots. This "ethnic awareness" seems to me to be much more a Canadian than an American phenomenon.

In most "ethnic" Canadian writing, and this is definitely true of Italian-Canadian literature, the ethnicity of the author legitimizes the credibility of the narrative and establishes a relationship between character and author based on ethnic identity. In contrast, texts by Italian-American writers like Rita Ciresi, Cris Mazza, Rose Romano, and Agnes Rossi erase the Italian background of both their authors and their characters, indicating distrust of ethnic memory. Most Italian-Canadian texts, on the other hand, including *The Lion's Mouth*, validate ethnic memory. It is his ethnic memory that helps Gianni survive in Bianca's first story. The narrator describes him as someone, who, unlike the doomed heroine in the story, retained "gentle memories, old customs and habits" (108). In like manner, the narrator's own ethnic memory aids her success.

The need for acknowledging the past calls for its critical re-examination and is not to be confused with nostalgia. By believing in her ability to write the "truth" about Marco/her Italian self, Edwards, through her narrator, demonstrates that ethnic "truth" is in narration. To become "whole" (or "androgyneous"), the narrator/Edwards needs to be able to feel comfortable in both her "inner city"/Venice (59) and her "outer city"/Edmonton (60).

> The title of this essay was inspired by the title of Ron Marken's essay given above.

NOTES

1. Early colonial writers, by contrast, tended to focus on colonial deficiencies.
2. Margaret K. Butcher argues that the pairing of male and female protagonists in the *Bildungsroman* is a technique found in a number of Commonwealth *Bildungsromane* and represents "a transitional stage in the development of the female as protagonist in her own right" (255).
3. Edwards also rewrites other gothic stock devices such as the discovery of the mysterious manuscript with the aunt's illegible letter, and the idea of the sins of the fathers visiting on the children with Marco's belief in being responsible for his son's heart disease.

WORKS CITED

Bakhtin, Mikhail. *The Dialogic Imagination: Four Essays*. ed. Michael Holquist. Trans. Caryl Emerson and Michael Holquist. Austin: U of Texas P, 1987.

———. *Rabelais and His World*. Trans. Helene Iswolsky. Bloomington: Indiana UP, 1984.

Butcher, Margaret K. "From *Maurice Guest* to *Martha Quest*: The Female *Bildungsroman* in Commonwealth Literature." *World Literature Written in English* 21.2 (1982): 254-62.

Di Michele, Mary. "Conversations with the Living and the Dead." *Language in Her Eye: Writing and Gender by Canadian Women Writing in English*. eds. Libby Scheier, Sarah Sheard, and Eleanor Wachtel. Toronto: Coach House Press, 1990. 100-06.

Edwards, Caterina. *The Lion's Mouth*. Montreal: Guernica, 1993.

Goodman, Charlotte. "The Lost Brother, The Twin: Women Novelists and The Male-Female Double *Bildungsroman*." *Novel* 17.1 (1983): 29-43.

Kreisel, Henry. *The Betrayal*. Toronto: McClelland and Stewart, 1964.

Marken, Ron. "Edmonton vs. Calgary: The Whole Truth." *Canadian Content*. Eds. Nell Waldman and Sarah Norton. Toronto: Harcourt Brace, 1996. 206-08.

Thurston, John. "Rewriting *Roughing It*." *Future Indicative: Literary Theory and Canadian Literature*. Ed. John Moss. Ottawa: U of Ottawa P, 1987. 195-204.

The Social Construction of Subjectivity in The Lion's Mouth

Marino Tuzi

Caterina Edwards' novel, *The Lion's Mouth*, depicts displacement and the process of adjustment from the perspective of the daughter of immigrant parents. The protagonist-narrator, Bianca Mazzin, is able to enter mainstream society, despite its intolerance of cultural difference. The experience of reaching adulthood in Edmonton and her questioning of the gender role assumptions of Canadian and Venetian society alleviate her cultural marginalization. While gender is an important component of her identity formation, Bianca implies that it is underlying social processes and not just patriarchy itself which shape the attitudes of men and women and their relations to each other. Instead of an antagonistic view of Italian and Canadian culture, the protagonist believes that both men and women constantly invent and reinvent their gender roles to meet social expectations. In doing so they become captive to the very ideas and behaviour that they no longer deem acceptable. As her postcolonial narrative indicates, an individual is not simply the product of external forces. Through personal choice, however limited it may be, one can have a measure of control over her life.

The Social Construction

In *The Lion's Mouth*, ethnicity is made up of many subject-positions which are attached to a varied, arbitrary, and frequently discrepant grouping of culturally-based beliefs and attitudes. This indeterminacy is represented through the employment of various formal techniques which destabilize the possibility of closure. The reflexivity of storytelling, in which the protagonist-narrator provides a commentary on the production of her text, broadcasts in part the conscious and incessant invention and reinvention of ethnicity and femininity. The rewriting of the past, of stories about life in the old country, and about immigration and adjustment in the new society serves a curative purpose (Kroetsch, 89).

Juxtaposition, such as the continual intercutting between Bianca's and Marco's stories, highlights the ambiguities and multi-layeredness of the protagonist's subjectivity as she moves back and forth between two divergent and elaborate cultural contexts. Remembrance, infused with a nostalgic/elegiac tone, exposes the discontinuities of history and subverts the essentializing of ethnicity. The social construction of cultural and gender identities, which is central to the study of this novel, is communicated through the leitmotif of performance, of role-playing, of masking and unmasking, and of the act of artifice-making. References to social history, such as immigration and political unrest in Venice, suggest that ethnicity derives from specific, conflicting, and always-changing material conditions. Underlying these formal techniques is the ironic mode which subtly profiles the unending inconsistencies and complexities of identity formation (Tuzi, 19-32).

Reflexivity and Storytelling

By composing her autobiography and in recreating the life of Marco Bolcato, her cousin in Venice, Bianca examines the suppositions of two opposed cultures and reveals to the reader the contingencies and disjunctions of ethnicity. In the process of writing her double narrative, Bianca presents past versions of these two stories. In each version, the protagonist comments directly on the production of her work, constantly providing extra-textual information and the motivations for her writing. The novel also suggests that her writing is influenced by external and contentious forces which prevent a congruous depiction of lived experience. Italian-Canadian identity is represented as something that is socially produced, continually changing shape and perspective as it shifts in and out of personal, social, and historical contexts. The multi-texturedness, stylization, and symbolic nature of the Venetian story further imply that identity is contrived and imagined. The narrator-character borrows from a variety of literary genres – shown in the use of romance, melodrama, espionage – and treats characterization, imagery, symbolism, and atmosphere as a means of conveying states of mind and cultural viewpoints. This conscious literariness contests the sort of writing that relies on the reconstruction of personal and social histories. It counters the supposedly epistemological aim of the storytelling: "I want to be the one who not only knows but illuminates the truth" (Edwards, 10). All the characters in the novel, at times even the protagonist-narrator herself, are presented as figures of the imagination. The reflexivity of the novel, evident in Bianca Mazzin's self-consciousness in telling her story and in the literariness of her Venetian narrative, emphasize the constructedness and indeterminacy of the ethnic subject. Each attempt to assemble the two narratives is contradictory and uncertain. In the first version, at the age of fifteen, Bianca fashions a sombre picture of a lonely and isolated Italian immigrant girl. Her cousin, Marco "who represented Venice lost" (75), inspires memories of a beloved country, but ultimately fails to save "the doomed heroine" from her predicament. While the protagonist-narrator tries to simplify the meaning of the story, remarking that it "illuminates the depth of the shock my family's emigration from Venice to Canada caused" (76), its underlying ambivalence refutes such a view. The inconsistent depiction of the Venetian cousin conveys a strong urge to return home and foreshadows her disillusionment with Venetian culture. Cultural transmutation issues in a conflicting portrayal of the old world.

In the second version, heroic images of Marco Bolcato are corroded by hints of moral turpitude and by allusions to deception and betrayal: "she was seduced and abandoned by the European, set on the path of her destruction" (108). The teen-aged Bianca still resists assimilation even as she spurns what she considers to be her parents' ossified ways. Sidelined by both cultures, Bianca invents a multicultural character who unites her North American and European identities: "She was a Joan Baez look alike, travelling in Europe. Her main characteristic . . . was her innocence" (108). The third version magnifies the paradoxical nature of ethnicity by overlayering contrasting images of the two cultures. The story of a woman who sees the shortcomings of her Venetian heritage as she builds a home for herself in the Canadian West is juxtaposed against inferences of a socially intolerant and largely unformed new society. Again, Marco is an embodiment of this complicated rendering of the process of identity formation in the new world: "So although you were made to represent the flaw . . . you did not carry all the blame" (144). Integration into the host country, which, in Bianca's early twenties, occurs through choice and the force of circumstance, produces a mixed identity. Although this multiplicity is figured in the image of a heroine who is "a Canadian girl with a Venetian background" (144), the key referent is the old world. The excesses of Bianca's Venetian fantasy indicate the extent of her discomfiture with the insularity of immigrant culture and the unimaginativeness of a Western Canadian lifestyle: "I gave my heroine wondrous acid trips through the history of Venice . . . I also gave her . . . lovingly detailed sex scenes. 'Gianni' and 'Serena' were lusty and inventive, coupling in unusual places and positions" (144). The hedonistic solipsism of the central character mirrors Bianca's fierce craving for a time before cultural transformation. It also ironically intimates an anxiety-ridden feminine sexuality, which transposes images from North American popular culture onto scenes from Italian photoromances. At the same time, it suggests the sensuality and decadence of the old world. The ancient city is an overdetermined trope for it signifies the intensity of Italianness, the unrecoverability of a lost identity, the primality of human appetites, and the onset of social decay. This third version of Bianca's novel is likewise disjunctive in its representation of Canada as a place which culturally marginalizes the protagonist yet cushions her against the stress of living in a traditional Italian household and releases her creative energy. The narrative studiously eschews a binary opposition of cultures and exploits the ambiguity of conflicting tendencies.

The paradoxes which suffuse all three stories inform the problematic of ethnicity and foreground Bianca Mazzin's conscious and habitual reframing of her identity. As she herself acknowledges, ethnicity is challengingly intricate and infinitely variable: "downfalls, no matter what the kind, were complex, difficult" (144).

The self-reflexivity of the storytelling is strengthened by the use of distancing devices and an interventionist narrative voice. The didacticism of the protagonist nullifies the dramatic tension of the narrative. She revisits events from the past to advance specific viewpoints that she maintains in the present. The story of her relationship with Jack, which turns into a social commentary on male and female conditioning, suggests that the inadequacy of gender roles results in the decision to leave her boyfriend. The protagonist's intercession shows a lack of sentimentality and is an attempt to guide the reader since she interprets the scene as it unfolds in past time. This distancing technique recurs throughout the narrative, such as in the criticism of her parents' refusal to give up archaic traditions and embrace modern Italian values: "They would not acknowledge that habits and guidelines could have changed in Italy since their youth. They clung to 'their way,' but disconnected from the society it expressed" (108). Bianca also addresses the reader who is ostensibly her cousin. Underneath the specific "you" is the implied reader of the text, whose expectations of a realist narrative often are left unfulfilled so that the reader, like Bianca, can critically assess the issues that are being presented. The narrator's interventions reflect her self-estrangement; although she describes emotions and details from the past, she moves outside them, as if she is scrutinizing the behaviour of someone else.

Reflexiveness prevents narrative closure. Both stories which the protagonist now presents to the reader indicate another permutation of identity. As Francesco Loriggio observes: "When [Bianca] finishes the new draft we cannot know whether she has been faithful to [Marco] or whether she has once more arranged his life to suit her present state of mind, as she did on previous occasions" (35). Each subsequent version of her story-within-a-story, which is a narrative in-process, invalidates the previous one as an approximation of the truth, since it delineates a radicalizing of perspective. The changeability of experience challenges the communicatory function of language, evident in the statement that "words . . . are things to be wrestled with, to be forced into the proper order" (48).

The problem with language is symptomatic of the difficulty of defining oneself in a volatile, culturally multi-tiered, and conflicted social environment. *The Lion's Mouth* implies that it is not just the linguistic difference between Bianca and Marco which causes estrangement but also the divergence of viewpoints. Storytelling is about the manufacturing of reality from the perspective of the writer: "I look out through your eyes. I become you. I make the story, the book" (180).

Fictiveness and a concomitant interpretive elasticity forestall narrational closure: "With me, it is always stories. And in the end it is all I can offer you" (180). The diverse characterizations of the Italian cousin repeats the contradictory action of the ethnic subject as she self-consciously reappropriates and rejects parts of her Italian heritage.

THE SOCIAL CONSTRUCTION   63

In her imagination, a sensitive and creative Marco energetically embraces the care-free lifestyle of Venice: "the city was the ancient way . . . the enjoyment that lay in the expanses of unfettered time" (148). The romanticizing of the ancestral culture is subsumed by images of a cynical and severely depressed individual who is divorced from the world around him. Cultural absence and the randomness of social contact underlie this inconsistent characterization of the Venetian: "I lay out a photo snapped by a sidewalk cameraman . . . we seem two strangers, caught in the frame by chance" (120).

Bianca's narrative of Western Canada is equally disjunctive and provisional. Arrival in the host country is emotionally and psychologically disabling even "though I was with Mamma and Papa, I felt stripped of family, of friends, of familiar walls and buildings . . . I was exposed, alone in the nothingness" (77). Compared to the refulgent Venetian landscape, the prairies are monotonous and "desolate" (76), especially in the interminable winter months.

Acculturation, however, proves to be exceedingly contradictory and discordant. While Bianca eloquently elevates the enormous potential of the new society, she is often on her guard because she thinks that the new world is inclined to place utilitarianism and materialism above human values. Anticipating the unproductive use of government funds at the inauguration of a constructed waterfall, her reservations quickly disappear at the beauty of its design and motion which recall fleeting images of "the [fabled] watery city" (179). Edmonton is perceived simultaneously as orderly and innovative and as "precarious, even transitory, an imposition rather than a natural growth" (47). It is an island in an oceanic sweep of prairie and economically and socially impermanent: "So many are here to take what they can. When the boom slackens . . . they will pack up their buildings and move on to a new camp" (47). The amassing of quick profits implies that the possibility of community-building is not just doubtful but ultimately illusory.

As in other postcolonial narratives Bianca sees industrial capitalism as mercilessly exploiting and constantly endangering the natural environment. Bianca's paean to the wilderness is undermined by the insinuation that nature is totally circumscribed and visibly altered by technological-urban society: "even though . . . I can hear the roar of trucks on the nearby thoroughfare and almost smell the noxious fumes, in a minute I can lose myself to the ravine woods . . . [to] the . . . sound . . . of the running water and of the birds and squirrels in the trees, where the only smell is the scent of pine or wildflowers (47). Disillusioned with modern Venetian society, the protagonist joins the immense potential of Western Canada to the pioneering spirit of her ancient ancestors, who "through their industriousness and will created joy from a barren marsh" (179). The amalgamation of cultures, of shaping the "vast spaces" and learning "the habit of art" (179), inspires an idealization of the host country, in which the immigrant constitutes from the materials of European culture a new and incorruptible community and identity. The new world, like the old, however, is an imaginative construct, for it exists only as a projection of what the protagonist considers to be possible.

Storytelling works against the forming of a coherent identity and, unwittingly, enacts the tensions and complexities of the Italian-Canadian subject. The protagonist as writer expresses her attachment to the new land while ensconced in her room and isolated from the community that surrounds her. Ethnicity is highly mutable, open-ended, and yet to be realized imaginatively: "Canada, out there . . . this terrain, is also here, in us, uncreated, evolving" (Itwaru, 19). Conventional storytelling, the ordering of disparate details into a comprehensible whole, cannot overcome linguistic and cultural differences: "I cannot write it in Italian, and you do not read English. I will never touch you at all" (180). The instabilities of traversing two opposed cultural fields are apparent in the continual revising of Marco's story: "As I look over those three earlier novels, I see that my changing needs, my shifting perceptions and understanding, cast you in different forms" (46). Immigration also challenges the fixity of cultural systems. Venice is amorphous, usually shrouded in ambiguity: "never this direct, cheerful shine but always a reflection flickering up from the canal" (46). The new world is as ephemeral and tenuous as the old and Edmonton "seems precarious, even transitory" (47).

JUXTAPOSITION

The juxtaposing of two stylistically different narratives, that of Bianca and her cousin, Marco, seems to inscribe an opposed set of cultural relations. The disorienting effect of this juxtaposition mirrors "the shock" of "emigration" when the protagonist's "life was split into two seemingly inimical halves" (76). First-person narration, made immediate by its didacticism and self-reflexiveness, transmits the protagonist's commitment to the re-defining of identity in Canada. In Marco's story, the distancing effect of omniscient narration is bolstered by the use of irony. Omniscience facilitates a critical stance and underlines the alterity of the Venetian subject. The ironizing of the characters' socio-political positions exposes a network of complicity and deception. While Marco is repelled by the vulgar commercialism of his employer, his complacent middle-class life is dissociated from the harshness of socioeconomic realities. Elena's revolutionary activity is motivated as much by the need to fashion a new identity after the collapse of her childhood dreams as it is by her concern for the plight of the powerless. This political posturing is opposed to Bianca's social commentary whose aim in exposing the shortcomings of both Italian and Canadian culture is to posit an alternative and progressive way of life. References to history, culture, and politics confirm the relativity and moral turbidity of Venetian society.

Present time and the lack of a consistent chronology in Bianca's autobiography invokes the urgency, dynamism, and open-endedness of identity formation. In contrast, Marco's story transpires in past tense with a more linear sequencing of events and is interspersed with flashbacks. The narrative's short time period, which commences on Friday afternoon and ends on Sunday night, lends an intensity to Marco's state of crisis. Unlike the protagonist's story which is about an identity in process, Marco's narrative depicts a life that has already run its course. Recurrent flashbacks usually conjure up images of a traumatic past, such as the bombing of the city of Zara during the Second World war or the breakdown of his marriage to Paola. This imagery suggests a society without hope or a future. The present tense in Bianca's autobiography hints at fluidity and possibility while past time in the Venetian narrative underscores personal and collective stagnation. The use of montage and the continuous intercutting between two narrative movements, give us a glimpse of the different sensibilities which have formed the two characters' identities.

Another technique is the jarring juxtaposition of literary genres. Autobiography, characterized by a measured self-reflection, clashes with a spy story which veers towards psychodrama. The thematic pattern of the Venetian narrative, which includes sexual and political subterfuge, adultery, betrayal, and eventual breakdown, suggests a world of moral ambiguity and shifting allegiances. Other elements of the pot-boiler – a feeling of constant menace, the use of character-types, such as a femme fatale and an unsuspecting hero, the use of an expressionistic setting, evocative of claustrophobia and decay, and the depiction of psychological and physical violence – systematically embody the frayed mental state of the protagonist, Marco Bolcato. The Venetian narrative is like a morality play in which the central character, after satiating his sexual appetite in the arms of a manipulative ex-lover, confesses his sins and accepts punishment through self-immolation. Moral clarity is subverted when Marco's consciousness, presented in the third person, melds with the voice of the assassin as victim and victimizer to become part of the same subjectivity.

The stylistic thrust of the text tilts against such narratological separateness and the opposition of cultural identities. Bianca's brief appearances in the story she is telling – as an adolescent who is infatuated with her charming but weary cousin – means that she too is a character-type.

This recourse to self-fictionalization problematizes the historical credibility of her autobiography. In the text, the protagonist is a literary construct, not just a mimetic representation of a particular subjectivity. The conscious fictionalization of one weekend in Marco's life, which borrows from the spy genre, also blurs the boundaries between biography and artifice-making. The two stories collapse into themselves and become figments of the protagonist's imagination. Also, as narrator, Bianca blends her subjectivity with that of her cousin. She inserts herself inside his head, so that he speaks through her. The compression and contraction of time in the novel are such that the first-person narration spans almost an entire life while the story of Marco unfolds over a two-day period. This compression coupled with the use of the present tense for the narrator's story and the past tense for Marco's counteracts the text's normal shift to linearity and cohesiveness. The double narrative is an index of the conflict and plurality of living at the nexus of contending cultural discourses. The two cultural identities of the protagonist constantly interact but remain contiguous, always resisting unification. The text also endorses the view that there is no essentialist Italian consciousness since it is perpetually altered by changing social forces. Venetian culture is over-layered with a largely symbolic Renaissance heritage as it ignites under the pressure of competing interests. Sentimentality verging on delusion and an inbred self-destructiveness partly activated by guilt characterize the text's representation of Marco Bolcato as a modern Venetian. In Canada, imported modes of behaviour ensure the survival of the immigrant while the exigencies of adjustment modify elements of the origi-

The Social Construction 69

nal culture. Italian-Canadian identity must be negotiated through a set of obstacles, whether it is the mainstream's cultural intolerance –"The worst transgression of all was my writing of Italy" (152) – or the limitations of a patriarchal-matrifocal family. The arithmetic of losses and gains produces anxiety, self-doubt, and precarious cultural allegiances. "Italianness" is a provisional gesture, for although it allows the protagonist to proclaim her ethnicity, it is profoundly unfixed and multifarious.

Memory

Historical realities impede the recuperation of a singular identity through the enactment of memory. Memory is not coherent, continuous, or seamless, but a sliding scale of contradictions and indeterminacies: "Venice, stone and water, Venice bride of the sea, bride of my dreams; she is the recurring motif that I cannot escape and I cannot capture" (175). The protagonist believes that European civilization can escape the ravages of the past by becoming part of a new society that is not constrained by history. In contrast, Marco Bolcato, who is haunted by horrific scenes from the past and who succumbs to the nihilism of history, confirms that there is no present or future, only an endless repetition of dead time. This binarism, this opposition between the lack of history in the new and the long and tragic history of the old, is undermined by allusions in the Venetian narrative to inner, inexplicable forces which transcend history, and by the historicizing of Canada as a product of European presence, of the adoption of old world ingenuity and cultural patterns.

The postcolonial narrative, moreover, insinuates that capitalist enterprise based on resource extraction has had a strong negative impact on the historical and social development of Alberta. The new moment is itself caught between two shifting cultural frameworks, which affect each other but resist homogenization. The narratives of the "I" and "Other" represent the various interacting but differentiated cultural perspectives of the protagonist. Such diversity undermines the essentializing project of memory and ushers in an irreducible and unrecoverable personal history.

Memory also ostensibly heralds the end of one historical period and the beginning of another. Bianca's early days in Venice and her subsequent return visits after she emigrates to Canada are set against a dynamic, colourful, and creative culture. Recollections of boisterous and energetic crowds during summertime and of the city with its endless canals, shops, and squares sentimentalize the past. As Bianca slowly becomes assimilated, she delineates the dark side of modern Venetian society, emphasizing the connection between its current problems and a decadent and often oppressive history. Haunted by guilt, shame, and self-loathing Marco is surrounded by a morally questionable social order which supplants memories of a young, jubilant, and idealistic man. Memory summons up a time before innocence was lost – before personal, cultural, and spiritual disintegration. Memory anticipates the demise of the old way of life and signals the protagonist's growing allegiance to the host country.

The elegizing of the old world is contradictory since ethnicity entails the reappropriation of the original identity at the same instant that Canadianness is being embraced. Ethnic subjectivity is not dichotomous and fixed but multiple and changeable. It encompasses past, present, and differing versions of its immigrant side while perpetually reforming itself in a complex and heterogeneous Canadian society. Remembrance is highly unstable since it is part of a field of experience that is contradictory and provisional.

Role Playing

Bianca continually assumes, deconstructs, and reconstructs her adverse and interlocking cultural identities: "Old masks replaced by new? The vision of the outsider, Italian, American, or [Western] Canadian, superseded by that of the native?" (48). The natural landscape, indefinable and mutable, complements the performance of newly acquired social roles: "the emotional slide . . . that coloured the country oppressive and infinitely barren, flipped up and back to be stored; a new one that painted the land familiar and supporting clicked into place"(48).

Role-playing, however, is often shaped by forces outside the control of the protagonist. The cultural homogeneity of the educational system, from public school to university, makes Bianca the focus of cultural discrimination, for "the circle [was] closing around me . . . We don't want DP's" (78), and tends to relegate her to the margins of social activity. Assimilative pressures result in the conscious appropriation of new self-images and viewpoints, evident in her longing "for ski jackets, jeans, shiny plastic shoes like everyone else's" (79), and appreciation of nature, which invigorates her and gives her a sense of solace and peace.

Canadian identity is formed as much by reacting against the belief system of Italian culture as it is by adapting to the social structures of the mainstream. Underneath Bianca's hostility to her ethnicity and her parents is the suggestion that only by moving out of the immigrant enclave and attaining a university degree, which she finances without family help, can she improve her social standing.

Mainstream society is inaccessible in part because it is colonized and fragmented: "[My country] was hidden, obscured. The history, the literature I was taught was English or American. The TV, the movies, the model for life was strictly American" (146). It is also inaccessible because ethnicity is multiple and diffused and therefore it is unable to position itself securely within any specific cultural context. The protagonist insists that she cannot animate her Italian traits, cannot "loosen the jaw. My mouth [cannot] open wide enough to let the words properly roll" (85), because "[t]he Canadian style ... had been coded into my body and could not be unlearned" (85).

"Canadianness" is not mere contrivance, "the mask" (84) which is superimposed on her Italian self, but a constituent part of her subjectivity. Likewise, while Venetian attitudes are socially constructed, they still influence the protagonist's perceptions of herself. Bianca identifies her physical appearance with that of the women in Longhi's paintings even though she realizes that such images are idealizations of a particular kind of Italian femininity.

The collision of intercultural perspectives produces an unstable and inconsistent ethnic subject. Immigration, assimilation, and ethnicization involve the appropriation, jettisoning, reappropriation, and reinvention of cultural identities. "Italianness" is separate from and coexists with "Canadianness."

As the protagonist's narrative indicates, ethnicity locates itself in several conflicting social orders at once. At the same time Bianca professes that she has harmonized her warring identities, she acknowledges the cleavage between herself and Marco. The transgression of cultural boundaries generates a restive, self-conscious, and complex identity. The self-consciousness of the ethnic subject is communicated through the leitmotif and imagery of performance, of the continual act of masking and unmasking.

The identities of the Italian characters are not represented as natural, static, or universal. Behaviour and outlook are affected by historically-specific and everchanging social relations. In the Venetian narrative, the image of the mask, which signifies the arbitrary construction of assigned roles, is foregrounded in the reference to *Carnevale*. This age-old festivity, wherein people don various masks and costumes, legitimates the discarding of prescribed roles, the removal of social and class barriers, and the open expression of desire. "[C]arnival celebrated temporary liberation from the prevailing truth and from the established order," argues Mikhail Bakhtin, "it marked the suspension of all hierarchical rank, privileges, norms, and prohibitions"(10). During the merrymaking, Marco Bolcato is surrounded by a sea of masks, by shifting and unplaceable identities: "He knew them and did not know them . . . [their physical appearance] seemed random details rather than identifiable characteristics" (89).

The mask as an overdetermined sign makes obvious the deception and impermanence of culturally-created identities. The central character is repeatedly invested with theatrical characteristics. Not only is role-playing uncertain, for "no matter what mask he chose for himself, others saw him only in subordinate roles" (66), but it is also improvisational: "he felt as if he had stumbled upon a stage . . . Both he and [the audience were] waiting for the action to begin" (37). The execution of his spousal role is both steadying and disorienting: "[His wife] was part of him and yet not part . . . she seemed utterly strange, utterly alien to his flesh" (154). Self-images transmit the absurdity and grotesqueness of a socially imposed identity: "His own face in the mirror was ridiculous; bulbous nose, sunken cheeks – a comedy mask, worst a gargoyle" (140). Other people deliberately act out their designated part, such as when his supervisor, Raponi, begins "to play the role for which he had been cast" (17).

Theatrical masks evoke the banality and one-dimensionality of facial features: "Marco . . . had the feeling he was facing not two human faces but the . . . masks of comedy and tragedy" (18). Role-playing turns people into functions, like the medical doctors, the masked men, who treat Marco's ill son with detachment. The enigmatic Elena personifies the factitiousness of public personas: she appears to him alternately as a cheap, worn-out, and sinister imitation of a sexpot, and as a sensual and breathtaking woman.

Powerful external conditions negate the development of an integrated personality. History is not continuous but disjunctive and destabilizing, exemplified in the ways that the brutality and horror of the World War II have restructured Marco's identity. By internalizing his physical and psychic pain, evident in his dark thoughts, self-hate, and guilt, Marco compulsively reenacts his victimization: "he must finish his role, he must make his denunciation" (171). His face acquires the mask-like aspect of the lion, *"Bocca di leone*, the starched mouth in agony without end" (172). The theatricality of the image confirms the performance-based nature of cultural identity.

Venice is the site of contending social, historical, and material forces. Since the city's inception, its inhabitants have been engaged in an endless combat with the elements: "Unceasing work, unceasing struggle, were essential in shoring up the 'frail barrier' . . . against the claims of the sea" (93). The ancient city was once a splendid and culturally sophisticated place, emblematic of the achievement of European civilization: "Two thousand years of history: Greek, Byzantine, Gothic, Baroque, coexisting in harmonious balance, a melody of man's potential" (104). It now is threatened by the deadly onslaught of commerce and industry. Ancient structures are levelled to make way for commercial enterprise, such as "a new resort complex on the Lido" (16). The gradual deterioration of irreplaceable architecture demonstrates the insidious effects of pollution. Political corruption and instability, subversive activity, sporadic bombings aimed at civilians, and politically-motivated assassinations have turned the city into a war zone. Underlining this decline are references to historical moments, primarily the Renaissance and the Second World War, which are suffused with images of oppression and extreme violence. Yet, as the text implies, Venice perseveres, continues to honour its traditions, continues in its indomitable manner to find creative solutions to difficult problems while cultivating a finely-textured lifestyle.

Social and historical discontinuity is communicated

through a series of contradictory and indeterminate images. Venice is composed of shimmering surfaces, of false fronts, of stunning architectural facades and of unspeakable and horrible realities: "[the] palace . . . appeared ethereal, a pink and white fantasy. How well it masked the inner warren of rooms and dungeons that was once the city's core of power"(15). The literariness of the images of Venice as a place of stone and water, which allude to John Ruskin's study of the fabled city, emphasize its artifice-making quality. The ancient citadel, anthropomorphized in the form of Elena who "encompassed the city" (62), is also depicted as being tantalizingly "beautiful" but ultimately made up of lethal "illusions" (62) which hide the evil that is slowly consuming its soul. The contradiction is supplemented with images of a luminous, exotic, and vibrant city and through a description of social unrest, decay, stasis which foreshadow impeding doom. Such provisionality rehearses the decentred subjectivities of Marco and the other characters: "Venice doubled and the three of them caught in the fulcrum on the doubleness" (138). Multi-faceted and highly fluid, the ancient city tenaciously resists closure: "Each stone in the city containing story over story, layer over layer of human history. Who could choose the essential one? The true one?" (170-171).

Gender Identities

The leitmotif of performance is also used in the representation of gender as a component of ethnicity. Gender is constructed by an aggregation of interconnected, antagonistic, and ever-changing social determinants. The novel shows how in Canada, "femininity" is defined from a clustering of opposed, disjunctive, and unstable cultural models. Mrs. Mazzin insists that her daughter Bianca should accede to patriarchal womanhood and renounce her fool-hardy independence. Helen Barolini claims that "[Italian immigrant] daughters assert a need for self-identity and want to free themselves from past patterns [but] in denying the value of the mother's role by their rebellion against it, they lay upon themselves a heavy and terrible conflict" (11).

The motif of the mask, of the illusoriness of cultural identities, resurfaces in the depiction of both traditional Italian and conventional Canadian femininity. Believing that her mother's "whole system of customs and beliefs was fake, a private fantasy, like the fairy tales" (84), Bianca assumes that the host society offers a more authentic and relevant form of femininity. The English-Canadian female role model she turns to proves to be contradictory and misleading. Jody's mother, an ostensibly genteel and open-minded woman, who functions as a wife and mother and is economically and socially dependent on her husband, differs little from her own mother, an unsophisticated working woman. North American popular culture actively promotes the values of conventional womanhood: "Loretta and I would . . . play out our latest fantasies with my Natalie Wood (her) and Sandra Dee (me) dolls" (80). Integration is hampered because the protagonist cannot accept the ideas and attitudes of a patriarchally-based English-Canadian society. Catholic school represses the protagonist's sexuality by associating desire with deviant and violent behaviour. The meaning derived by Bianca and her friends from the gory tale of St. Maria Goretti who chooses death over the loss of her virginity ironically confirms the power of female sexuality: "A martyr to foul male lust . . . Her very presence had inflamed a man to violence" (109-110). This implied reinterpretation of the story temporarily preempts Catholicism's disapproval of female desire: "Sex was a basic appetite like hunger and thirst, and the satisfying necessary . . . The church had mounted an enormous scaffold of lies to control and oppress" (110).

Popular femininity is shown to reside in an elitist, hierarchical social system. Distancing herself from Bianca in order to consolidate her status among the daughters of affluent families, Jody upholds the group's decision to reject a fellow student's membership because of her ethnicity and social class. The subsequent relationship with Jack, who is of Ukrainian background, opens Bianca up sexually and frees her from Italian womanhood but it also limits her to a socially sanctioned femininity. The coincidence of Jack's traditional ethnic values with the gender suppositions of the mainstream infers that patriarchy moves across cultural boundaries. By disclosing the sham of romantic love, the protagonist signals her resistance to the norms of the dominant culture: "the man and woman meet, they make love, they move in together, they discover indeed they are in love . . . he must be the much-awaited prince, she the lovely princess. There must be a happily-ever-after, a validation" (49). The pull of ethnicity at times supplants the appropriation of a new feminine self. Wanting to rekindle her bond with a sickly Marco, Bianca imaginatively assumes the role of the nurturer: "Hold your hand, iron your shirt, tempt you back to food with homemade pasta . . . I could soothe" (52). The story of Bianca's present life in Edmonton is played out against a backdrop of towering mountains and endless prairie. The allusions to a regenerative nature, which is linked to Bianca's creativity as a woman, hint at a curative feminine space.

This invocation of femaleness is part of the protagonist's story-making, and, as such highlights the conscious re-framing of identity and not the privileging of an essential femininity. Positioned within two mobile and incompatible cultural systems, the protagonist cannot unite her multiple feminine identities. Gender as a series of social guises likewise pervades the Venetian narrative. The characters frequently emulate media-generated images of masculinity and femininity. Piero, Elena's comrade and lover in the revolutionary underground, consciously imitates the stylized aggressivity of fictional detectives on American television. Marco's stilted perceptions of the women in his life reproduce the sexual dichotomies of patriarchal culture. The virginal image of Paola as "a magazine cover bride[,] [s]o perfect in her elegant lace and silk, in the pearl coronet and the cascading floor length veil" (30) is contrasted to a coquettish Elena dripping with lust: "She slowly slid off her white fur jacket, pursing her red, red lips into a girlie magazine pout"(58). These stereotypical images of women indicate Marco's complicity with patriarchy. As Elena performs her role as a temptress, objectifying her body, Marco indulges in "crude [sexual] fantasies" (62). The fabrication of gender identities is attached to a system of structured behaviour. Even after Elena sheds her disguise in the process of making love, Marco notes that "her reactions remained skilled, almost professional" (62). The emptiness of their lovemaking exposes the sterility of socially conditioned gender roles. Romantic love was "[the] surface titillation by programmed caresses, mental fantasies, or the vaporous sentiments of young lovers . . . [it was] the reflection of themselves in their lover's eyes that they loved . . . [it was] the postures, the trappings, the masks, they wanted" (100-101). Elena persists against sexual objectification and affirms the complexities of feminine identity: "behind her assigned role [she] became more fluid, more uncontainable" (62). Paola's refusal to be a domestic and sexual servant and the falsity of Marco's furtive liaison with Elena split open the distorting categories of patriarchy and reveal the arbitrariness and contigencies of masculinity.

Gender as socially defined is contexualized within the parameters of Western society. While citing the male-centrism of the old world, Bianca implies that a woman is similarly constrained by the patriarchal strictures of Canadian society: " 'One difference between here and there is the men. In Canada, among educated people particularly,' I was exaggerating, lying almost 'antiquated roles are passing away' " (150). Gender relations are portrayed as complex and contradictory. The female characters try to overcome their subordination by using their domestic functions to attain some leverage in their relationships or by openly repudiating traditional notions of womanhood.

Domesticity and motherhood, which are key components to the maintenance of family, contest the male's primacy, illustrated by Tarquinio's deference to his wife in establishing the priorities of the household and Marco's sense of inadequacy in coping with his son's debilitating illness. Elena, who has opted out of conventional womanhood by divorcing her husband and becoming involved in political subversion, strategically assumes subservient feminine poses in order to undermine male control, whether it is her lover Piero, whose macho posturing depends on the enactment of her female-based erotic/violent persona, or Marco, deluded in his belief that he can master her sexually. Bianca's representation of the male subject is similarly conflictive. Marco Bolcato operates in several categories simultaneously: his physicality and virility awaken young Bianca's adolescent desire, his sensitivity and emotionality give him an androgynous quality which transcends gender difference, his egoism, paternalism, and sexual infidelity confirm his patriarchal nature. Jack is likewise contradictorily depicted as a man who has an intuitive connection to the land and whose natural physical presence allows Bianca to effortlessly express her sexuality. Yet he is a hyper-rationalist and adheres to conventional masculine values. The protagonist's break up with Jack and her inability to communicate with her traditionally-minded cousin demonstrate her refutation of patriarchal masculinity: "Through her writing [Bianca] finds that . . . her identity cannot be bound up with that of a man. Individual freedom and independence, especially as she finds them in Western Canada, are important for Bianca's development as a person" (Pivato, 83).

Bianca's narrative deconstructs established images of femaleness and affirms her autonomy as a woman. Yet the male subject, ambiguously embodied by Marco, is integral to her self-conscious exploration of ethnicity. Like some other women in the postcolonial novel, Bianca unwittingly facilitates and vigorously subverts a partiarchally based maleness, blurring the line between victim and skilful opponent.

WORKS CITED

Bakhtin, Mikhail. *Rablais and His World*, trans. Helene Iswolsky. Cambridge: MIT Press, 1965.

Barolini, Helen. *The Dream Book: An Anthology of Writing by Italian American Women*. New York: Shocken Books, 1985.

Edwards, Caterina. *The Lion's Mouth*. Edmonton: NeWest Press, 1982; rpt. Toronto: Guernica, 1993.

Itwaru, Arnold. *The Invention of Canada*. Toronto: TSAR, 1990.

Kroetsch, Robert. "The Grammar of Silence," *The Lovely Treachery of Words: Essays Selected and New*. Toronto: Oxford University Press, 1989.

Loriggio, Francesco. "History, Literary History and Ethnic Literature," in *Literatures of Lesser Diffusion*. eds. J. Pivato, S. Totosy and M.V. Dimic. Edmonton: Research Institute for Comparative Literature, 1990.

Pivato, Joseph. "Italian-Canadian Women Writers Recall History," *Canadian Ethnic Studies* XVII, 1 (1986).

Tuzi, Marino. *The Power of Allegiances: Identity, Culture and Representational Strategies*. Toronto: Guernica Editions, 1997.

Cinderella Revisioned

The Female Persona in Caterina Edwards, Genni Gunn, and Mary di Michele

FRANK CAUCCI

In the repertoire of over one hundred and thirty versions of *Cinderella*, including Grimms' original and magical *Ashputtle*, and the realist *La cenerentola* of Rossini's opera, the diversity in variables from one version to another underscores the constancy of several leitmotifs. Among these are Cinderella's forced abandonment of her initial context, the injustice of her subsequent state and, not least of all, her discovery and ultimate rescue by a prince who will make her happy ever after. By divesting the Cinderella myth of its escapist axiology, while foregrounding the neo-realist tradition of Italian Canadian writing, we may consider a current application of these themes in the works of Caterina Edwards, Genni Gunn, and Mary di Michele.

Be it psychological, physical, or moral, abandonment is acutely present in Caterina Edwards' play, *Homeground*, where the characters share a sense of relinquishment to their individual unfolding. Female characters, particularly, suffer a sense of loss since they are dependent on their men through marriage. The image of a saturnalian homeland sacrificing its children renders best the characters' personal drama, a consequence of abandoned familial responsibility. This condition, articulated by Lucio when he complains that "even our damned homeland chose us as sacrifices to their contentment, their well-being" (35), is often echoed in Italian Canadian writing, as evidenced in the works of D'Alfonso, Di Cicco, Melfi, Micone, Ricci, Salvatore, among others.

Rooted in an Indian legend in an altogether different context, Genni Gunn's novel *Thrice upon a Time* begins with the mystery of an abandoned baby whose natural mother, herself abandoned at birth, investigates and then reconstitutes the history of four generations of ancestral lineage, at the head of which are two enigmatic matriarchs. Elise's subtext tells the story of these strong, autonomous women, providing information about her own identity and origin. While reconstructing her ancestral history, the heroine's complex of uprootedness surfaces unwittingly as she becomes cognizant of the abandonment motif punctuating her lineage. This motif is explicitly referenced in the title of the novel whose fairy tale allusion foregrounds the central theme of the Cinderella myth.

Mary di Michele's *Under My Skin* illustrates yet another example of the sense of loss through abandonment in forty-year-old Rita Chiddo, who continues to fantasize married life with Nikos ten years after their mock marriage. Her lover of a few months, whom she considers a good man – and a rarity – believes she clings to the image of Nikos only because it limits "the power of other men in her life" (28). Paradoxically, she is unable to love another man, settling for less significant bonding, as illustrated by her sexual but loveless relationship with her married boss.

The experience of loss through abandonment tends also to underscore the characters' uprootedness. In Edwards' *The Lion's Mouth*, the narrator-character acknowledges the shock emigration produces on her family, including her parents' difficult adjustment to the new land. Her very aloneness, her mispronunciation of English sounds and limited semantic grasp of the language, her status as a "DP" (78), constitute her own branding and sense of shame vis-à-vis her classmates.

The characters' uprootedness in *Homeground* makes it impossible for them to avoid scrutinizing the geography of place, long central to the thematics of Canadian literature. If it is true, as Robertson Davies has posited, that one of the Canadian writer's responsibilities is to show Canada to Canadians, then Edwards' heroine defines her relationship to the land from the perspective of the orphaned Cinderella. Raised by an aunt after her own mother dies giving birth to her, and forced to leave her village at the age of fourteen, Maria finds herself displaced to "a cold city, among strangers" (28). Her experience as an immigrant, first to Milan and later to Edmonton, reinforces her sense of abandonment and alienation. Maria's vision of "here" and "there," which she shares with the other *dramatis personae*, thus functions as a heuristic metaphor. The home country represents the scene of the Fall and subsequent banishment; the host country, geographic displacement and expiation.

Speaking of a fellow emigrant who dies in Whitehorse shortly after his arrival there, and echoing Candida's designation of Canada as a "God-forsaken place" (23), Maria blames his death on displacement: "I don't care what the coroner said. It was this country [. . .] To die so far from home" (11). Maria's metaphysical geography constitutes a dystopia central to her orphaned Cinderella imaginary. As Margaret Laurence once intimated, "When you have failed to establish physical or spiritual harmony with your environment, hostility is the only alternative to complete emptiness and unmeaning" (Jones 40).

In contrast to the here and now, *Homeground*'s two female protagonists express memories of an idealized village life. Mnemonic energy focuses on the lost object which, heightened by hindsight, now becomes coveted and is even attributed an overcompensation in the figure of hyperbole. Candida best describes this sense of loss when she shares with Maria her childhood ignorance about not knowing "how good everything was" (24). Edwards' characters evoke Frye and Atwood's thematics of the fortress mentality and of victimhood, perpetuating the quintessential Canadian literary identity of the split self and of duality first depicted in the works of Frances Brooke and Susanna Moodie, and shared in nineteenth century French Canadian literature.

The Lion's Mouth, too, goes back and forth between the narrator's yearning for a lost Venice and a more prosaic Edmonton, in the course of her final attempt at writing a novel about Marco. In the words of Michel de Certeau, what does such travel produce if not an exploration of the deserted places of one's memory, an uprooting of one's origins, a fiction with the double effect of displacements and condensations? Bianca's love of Marco and of Venice increases her sense of isolation, forcing the adolescent narrator to relate her Canadian ways to a persona, and identify her true self as Venetian, especially when placed between unaccepting peers who scorn her difference, and an unhappy mother confronted with her daughter's increasing Canadianness.

Uprootedness is manifest even at the level of the creative process. For when the narrator takes her manuscript to a writing school, she is admonished for writing about Italy, and urged to write about "here." In the end, this serves only to reinforce the narrator's vision of Western Canada, as alien to her as Venice is to her peers. "I wrote of Venice. I wrote of you, and still do, not from choice but need. We must each of us stare into the lion's mouth" (152), the narrator states allusively, for the lion's mouth is the repository of truth and vehiculates self-disclosure.

The title of *A Whiter Shade of Pale*, a novella by Caterina Edwards, is a reference to a Willie Nelson song that acts as catalyst for unleashing George's Proustian-style, involuntary memory of two summers spent as a student on an archeological dig in Rome. As memories of a happy, personal past abound in the character's stream of consciousness, the narrator also foregrounds his knowledge of a remote, Etruscan past in his fragments of recall: "The nerves in the ends of his fingers recognize the traces of human intention and will" (12). Place is displaced through an embedded structure, becoming twice removed from the story's original setting in Canada. Moreover, the double topographic and diachronic displacement in memory serves to redefine George's middle years in relation to his wife and marriage. In this way, the character undergoes an ensouling experience that allows him to reconsider who he was in order to understand better who he is at the present.

In *Becoming Emma*, another novella by Edwards, the heroine has been uprooted more than once: first to America from the old country, and then to Canada. She becomes an ex-patriot in Edmonton after following her husband who obtains a position as researcher at the University. She undergoes name changes from Aida to Sandra, before becoming Emma – a reminder of uprootedness as she assumes different personas in the course of her lifetime. The last of these, Emma is reminiscent of the Flaubertian prototype, although Edwards' narrator compromises unhappily between Emma Bovary and Austen's Emma Woodhouse. In becoming herself, Edwards' heroine thus shares with her nineteenth-century predecessors the need for a social construction. Like Cinderella, but with varying effects, they ultimately undergo a metamorphosis and achieve self-discovery.

Interspersed with Emma's unfolding is the story of Latvia's own uprootedness throughout a history of "conquest, subjugation and domination" (88). The authorial voice interrupts the narrative at essential intervals to report on the country's Russification and growing demographic imbalance since World War II. The threat to Latvia's identity is thus posited as a syntagmatic expression of domination and submission in tandem with Emma's character, which evolves from a position of strength (a promising artistic career) to one of perceived weakness (self-abnegating marriage and motherhood).

Uprootedness is therefore directly related to a loss of individual identity and memory. Assuming the roles of housewife, mother, facilitator, and caretaker for her borders in *Homeground*, for instance, Maria appears to suffer from symptomatic sensory aphasia. Reduced to the role of acolyte and unquestioningly silenced, she is unable to express herself or to acknowledge clearly her feelings, even before her psychologically weak husband. She clings to the old ways and to the tribal rites of her past, seeking solace and safety in them before her hostile environment. However, she cannot remember them. As in the Cinderella myth, the heroine's split with the past appears to be irrevocable.

Maria's relentless attempts at safeguarding a cosmogony of witchcraft evoke the archetypal wise woman as well as the Demeter myth, as illustrated by the strong bond with her newborn daughter. It also symbolizes the loss of a life-preserving, matriarchal, philogenetic past. This vestige of a collective unconscious informs her personal unconscious, which struggles to reconstitute itself, to become whole again and thus recover her loss. Contrary to the Cinderella outcome, however, such attempts at recovering the self's unity appear to be vain. In her journey towards individuation, Maria ultimately discovers what Foucault has posited regarding the ideology of return: namely, that a return to the past is only illusory. Faced with this truth, Maria realizes that the past may not be regained, and that unity may not be recovered.

It is significant that *Homeground* was first produced in 1986 as *Terra straniera,* foreign country, at the Edmonton Fringe Festival. The action takes place at Maria's boarding house, which serves as a cocoon for the old country by maintaining indefinitely the illusion of the past amidst the hostile environment of the new. As such, the characters' *home ground* is the prelude to their inevitable and unwitting transformation, a posteriori to the play. The poetics of this unintentional metamorphosis may be seen to originate with the emigrant's drive to redeem himself. To illustrate, Maria's conscientious response to Lucio's lament that the only jobs available entail brute labor and reduce the individual "to a beast of burden," is that an immigrant must buy his way out (16).

Clearly, the inversion of the myth of the American dream in *Homeground* works in counterpoint to the inversion of the myth of the past and of the homeland "which chose us as sacrifices to [its] contentment" (38). What remains is an existentialist sense of *huis clos* for, as Maria ultimately discovers, there remains neither the possibility of a return home, nor that of feeling at home. Lucio's words best echo this message when he posits that each one of us is alone; alone without escape (83).

The impossibility of return is the backdrop for Laura, too, in *Thrice upon a Time*. After wedding the hapless Henry upon docking in Victoria from England, she follows him through the wilderness to a mining shaft and witnesses the snow filling their footsteps as a constant erasing of the past (72). In this metaphor, the past is encased in the figure of a palimpsest. As for Rita's Italian roots in *Under My Skin*, these are relegated to "her dark-eyed inner self" (109). Di Michele's heroine also negotiates the past as palimpsest, for Rita has not been successful in safeguarding an ethnic identity beyond that of her father's culinary expertise.

To some degree or other, we may ascribe the nature of the heroines' partnerships and marital relationships to their uprootedness. In *Becoming Emma*, for instance, the heroine's boredom with her domesticity and her unrealized aspirations and fantasies are important factors leading her in the arms of Lamartine. As she bides her time, Emma's suspension casts her in the role of a number of popular, mythical heroines alluded to by the narrator. In this context, the wily Lamartine is the passing prince. When at last they consummate their relationship, the heroine's transformation into Emma appears to be complete – even as she faces her inevitable disillusionment.

In Genni Gunn's *On the Road*, the speaker's peregrinations with her band, from one town to the next, are rife with illusions in love. The very title of the collection of stories connotes this illusory idea and demonstrates that the impermanence of love relationships and the fragility of marriage are themes with a multiplicity of variations – as evidenced parodically in the title of one of the stories, "Endless Love." The narrator repeatedly illustrates a love "reduced to the politics of power, complete with deceptions, misconceptions, suspicions and, finally, the coming of a new acerbic jargon," that is, "the language of departure" (34). The nature of such short-term, nomadic relationships seems to be pre-established in a poem significantly titled "Departures." Here, Genni Gunn's persona retraces her father's odyssean-style wanderings and, as she comes "to expect the partings / the vigour of renewal" (44), she acknowledges that "forever and always have become finite / in my dictionary" (45).

In *Under My Skin*, Rita identifies strongly with her Italian-born father who immigrated to America as a child, and thus considers herself ethnic. She still resents her parents' failure to attend her wedding, especially since they were ignorant of its mock nature: "It would have been real, a real marriage, if they had made the trip to bless it" (63). She remains loyal to the memory of Nikos, whom she cannot have; refuses Barry's love and legitimate marriage proposal, and engages for several years in a non-threatening, sexual relationship with the womanizing Pierre Bilodeau. Even her friends concur that Rita's life is not anchored in reality, a characterization corroborated by the narrator: "Some people live more in their imaginations than in their real life. She was someone like that. She belonged in a movie where she was sure to fall in love with Spencer Tracey and be loved in return" (233). Such phantasies connote the fairy-tale leitmotiv of a heroine whose quest for ultimate union may only be realized upon being discovered by her prince.

The nature of the heroines' relationships appears to be closely grounded in considerations of gender. In most cases, the heroines are very conscious of their unenvious condition as women – a context reinforcing the position of noted feminist Eve Kosofsky Sedgwick, who argues that gender is a social construction. In *Homeground*, for instance, Candida relates the assigned role of both female protagonists to an old peasant proverb: "When a girl is born, a servant is born; when a boy is born, a lord" (27). Oppositional gender categories are thus established between female subservience and male dominance. The more outspoken of the two characters, Candida refers to the assignation of dominance to mankind and of subserviance to womankind as brainwashing. However, she is cognizant that this knowledge is not in itself sufficient to break the pattern.

In *Becoming Emma*, the narrator synthesizes the heroine's situation as "a common one for a mother of young children" (96). Emma considers herself a third-generation feminist "who having the mental freedom the older generation did not, was not interested in traditional female work: repetition, domesticity, boredom" (125). She rails at such Cinderella-type syllogisms as "the good girl married the prince and the bad girl burned to a crisp" (118), and at mythological markers in female socialization patterns in general.

This is also true of Bianca in *The Lion's Mouth*, where the Aphrodite archetype is active and recreates over and over in her imagination the moment she falls in love with Marco. Yet Bianca does not take the beauty myth seriously. When she sees the photos of herself – a reminiscence of Marco's and Elena's attempted transformation of her – she confesses that "she never looked like that before or after again," and that she "knew it was art, not reality" (119-20).

Discussing the question of literary models in *Becoming Emma*, the narrator concludes that the lot of women writing has indeed little to do with Flaubert's life as a writer, and a great deal more to do with Austen's. "*Flaubert, c'est moi?* Each time I pick up *Madame Bovary* again, I feel how unapproachable he is, the god-like author he wanted to be, everywhere present and nowhere visible. *Flaubert, c'est moi?* Get real, as my Emma would say" (178). At this late stage in the novel, Edwards' authorial presence no longer hesitates on the question of literary models: her identification with Jane Austen is complete.

In *On the Road*, the protagonist's mother has taught her certain cardinal rules about men. In her experience, a woman should practice flattery, weakness, intellectual servitude, and the withholding of sexual favours before submission (31). Without intending any irony, the narrator concurs with her mother's rules. In *Thrice upon a Time*, Elise describes her female lineage as able to achieve happiness, equality, and power through an independent mindset (24). This may be evidenced in the pagan archetype of the virgin which, when "dominant in a woman's psyche, the characteristic that is most noticeable in her relationship with others is that she is her own master" (Dunn Mascetti, 65).

Under My Skin also contains extensive references to women's servitude to men. Illustrations of this are probably most chilling when they relate to Dr. Skelton, according to whom, "women suffered from impaired right brain function" (133). One revealing episode has him snap into place the head of his daughter's stripped and decapitated Barbie doll with the same expert hands, one might add, he uses to strangle his female victims while raping them. Consequently, it is no surprise that his marriage to Lily has the effect of silencing her and of canceling her very existence. The sleeping pills he prescribes are intended to undermine her conscious awareness and to objectify her further. She is mindful of the desired effect through her identification with Scheherazade, "buying time with the small tale in each pill [. . .] so she might be reprieved for one more night" (210).

In the afterword to the novel she has just written, Rita Latte, whose feminist sensibilities parallel those of her heroine, calls herself Lady Lazarus before a patronizing boss who wishes only to seduce her. Just as the narrator of *Becoming Emma* addresses earnestly the question of a literary model for women in the novel's embedded story, Rita, too, is left to reflect on an appropriate role model for women. Her reflection ends ironically with the naming of two icons, which she uses in an attempt to subvert the patriarchal order: Cleopatra and Madonna. The real and substantive models remain buried in her intentional hiatus.

Clearly, the heroines in question do not live happily ever after. Realism precludes such artless endings. The axiological import of the Cinderella myth exposes the bedrock of our Western, patriarchal order. After all, Cinderella's natural grace is finally recognized, and wins the prince's favour – something her two half-sisters fail to do. In this perspective, the works discussed depart from the static compensation of the happily-ever-after ending, perverting the axiology's resolve. They do, however, share the discourse of uprootedness, abandonment, and the problematic acquisition of a different, conflicting persona and consciousness. In this context, Cinderella's survival is symptomatic generally of Italian Canadian literature since it is negotiated by a conflictual sense of belongingness. Her duality becomes manifest when she is cognizant of the erasure of her past. In the words of Margaret Atwood, the act of choosing Canada as the new *homeground* thus becomes "the choice of a violent duality" (62).

More specifically, the heroines of Caterina Edwards, Genni Gunn, and Mary di Michele tend to follow the Emmas of the world who live their lives in a state of flux, but fatefully endeavor to pursue their journey. The heroines' dynamic unfolding and fictional transformation ultimately reveal the forging of a new self-image, which includes the construction of gender identity.

WORKS CITED

Atwood, Margaret. *The Journals of Susanna Moodie*. Toronto: Oxford U P, 1970.

De Certeau, Michel. *The Practice of Everyday Life*. Berkeley: U of California Press, 1984.

Denham, P. and Edwards, eds. *Canadian Literature in the Seventies*. Toronto: Holt, Rinehart & Winston, 1980.

Di Michele, Mary. *Under My Skin*. Kingston: Quarry Press, 1994.
Dunn Mascetti, Manuela. *The Song of Eve: Symbols of the Goddess*. N.Y.: Fireside, 1990.
Edwards, Caterina. *A Whiter Shade of Pale*. Edmonton: NeWest, 1992; rpt: Toronto: Guernica, 1993).
_____. *Becoming Emma*. Edmonton: NeWest, 1992.
_____. *Homeground*. Montreal: Guernica, 1990.
_____. *The Lion's Mouth*. Edmonton: NeWest, 1982.
Foucault, Michel. *The Foucault Reader*. Paul Rabinov, Ed. N.Y.: Pantheon, 1984.
Gunn, Genni. "Departures." *Quarry Magazine*, 38, 2 (Spring 1989).
_____. *On the Road*. Ottawa: Oberon, 1991.
_____. *Thrice Upon a Time*. Kingston: Quarry Press, 1990.
Jones, D.G. *Butterfly on Rock*. Toronto: U of Toronto P, 1970.
Kosofsky Sedgwick, Eve. "Axiomatic," *Epistemology of the Closet*. Berkeley: U of California Press, 1990.

Research Notes on Edwards' Fiction
Pasquale Verdicchio

I believe that it is in Emilio Villa's silent tensions and Andrea Zanzotto's wintry linguistic regurgitations that we find a significant point of reference for Italian-Canadian writers. In a recent review of the work of two Italian-Canadian writers in the journal, *Canadian Literature*, Lesley Clement quotes a 1990 essay by Antonio D'Alfonso regarding a "third phase that will perhaps bring us back to the personal and political realm." By recognizing that a third stage was in fact now active, Clement provides a critical stance that far exceeds what most Italian-Canadian critics themselves have been willing to propose.

The major obstacle to a full appreciation of Italian-North American writing, both internal and external to the larger communities it encompasses, is the lack of historicization. While some critics suggest that it is a matter of functioning in an environment that offers no tradition, it is important to stress that no hyphenated writer emerges *tabula rasa* from the oyster shell of expatriation. Even if not rooted in North American soil, writers are inscribed by history and carry a catalogue of experience.

In her novella, *A Whiter Shade of Pale* (1992), Caterina Edwards deals with the nature of self-discovery and historicization through the persona of a (would-be) archeologist. The work is built around fragments of information and leaves much to the interpretation of these findings.

Nothing is complete and resolved. The reader is left to unveil layers of (someone else's) history: a child's sarcophagus (truncated history), an unmatched pair of earrings (discontinuous history). A juxtaposition of one's own unconscious graphia/writing, as represented by the patterns of the archeologist's recurring nosebleeds, to the body of graphic expression of the vanished Etruscans whose remains are being excavated, provides a way of comparing and constructing history.

George's frequent nosebleeds are described as "a random scattering of red dots on a white page"(8). The silent expression of the body that this image engenders threads a series of images and formal elements that go from the novella's title to the various literary quotes placed within the author's writing itself. The red dots appear as a scattering only because, as with Etruscan language, it is not "that their language is indecipherable ... It is understanding it that presents problems, since it is of unknown origin and cannot with certainty be related to any group of known languages"(Edwards, 1992, 1). The literary production of Italian-Canadian writers is squarely positioned in an uncertain relationship to both English and Italian traditions. For many, both are learned languages of foreign cultures. As such, the writing of Italian-Canadians cannot "with certainty be related to any other group of known languages." By establishing this type of questioning of languages, Italian Canadian writers cannot but come to the realization that, as George Sefaris suggests, "those statues are not the fragments. You yourself are the relic."

In the case of Caterina Edwards, her association with the Italian-Canadian writing group is particular, since her first identity signifier, her name, does not immediately suggest such an association. Her novella is particularly interesting because of the way in which Edwards continues her experiments with contextualization found in another one of her books, *The Lion's Mouth* (1982). In *A Whiter Shade of Pale* the sense of search and construction of context is more explicit. George is attracted to Etruscans precisely because he is unable to contextualize them. He himself seeks a decontextualized existence, a relationship to the world that offers continuously shifting terms of reference and interpretation (40-41). What is left behind or left over from the interpretative work in this novella are the protuberances of our life work that have broken off like the noses of the statues from the digs. These are the artifacts that provide a context for those who read our passage. Finally, as with the Etruscan writing that is "read but not understood"(43), one must ask one's self if this is the ethnic experience. Aging and memory (and not the artifacts of George's relationships) are the elements of hidden contextualization that we must decipher. A less explicit and obtrusive writing, whose signs of ethnicity are no less present, would enable us to outline some potential evolutionary trends in Italian-Canadian writing. In fact, Lesley Clement's terms of reference for her discussion of the "third stage" in Italian-Canadian letters are Caterina Edwards and myself.

While I provisionally accept Clement's reading of D'Alfonso's "third stage" designation, we should beware of the fact that it is not simply a stage in a progression. This "stage" which may be designated by style and linguistic experimentation exists concurrently with other "stages." What third stage writers illustrate is that no group is reduceable to any particular set of themes and modalities. The appearance of progress, evolution, and definition of stages may be a matter of generational distinctions or cultural distance from one's place of origins, language of choice, or other such variants, even if these are but a few of the determinants that influence a body of work.

> These notes are extracted from Pasquale Verdicchio's *Devils in Paradise* (Guernica, 1997), and suggest the many rich possibilities for further research into the work of Caterina Edwards and other women writers.

Works Cited

D'Alfonso, Antonio. "Where Do We Go From Here?" in *Writers in Transition*. eds. C.D. Minni & A. Foschi Ciampolini. Montreal: Guernica, 1990.

Verdicchio, Pasquale. *Nomadic Trajectory*. Montreal: Guernica, 1990.

_____. "Post-Emigrant Culture: Thoughts on Race, Ethnicity and the Politics of Disapperance," *The Toronto Review*, 16, 3 (1998), 23-34.

Villa, Emilio. *Opere Poetiche I*. Milano: Coliseum, 1989.

Zorzotto, Andrea. *Fosferi*. Milano: Mondadori, 1983.

A Short Note on *Becoming Emma*

Anna Pia De Luca

Aida Avendemis, the Latvian protagonist and former graphic artist in Edwards' 1992 novella *Becoming Emma,* is really not much different from Bianca Mazzin. But unlike Bianca, Aida initially rejects her Latvian roots, preferring to be a naturalized American living in Edmonton with all its trappings and tedious household boredom. It is only after a series of name changes and life styles based on her reading of Austen's Emma Woodhouse and in particular Flaubert's Emma Bovary, that Aida, who for many years had now been calling herself Emma, awakens to the realization that her past must be dealt with, lived with, and not wiped out.

The narration offers various dialogical levels where Aida's past is superimposed on her present and past and present are interfaced with the fictive lives of her namesakes, thus permitting the reader not only to observe Aida's many transformations, but above all to perceive the subtle innuendoes of Edwards' subversive female text. The chapters unfolding Aida's story are also followed by narrative interpolations, where Edwards inserts brief glimpses of Latvian history and uses the world of pictorial and ficticious art, along with authorial critical interpretations of the techniques of writers and painters of the past, to underline the possibilities of alternate readings of truth.

The Emma we meet at the beginning of the novella, with three children and a busy academic husband working in Edmonton, like Bovary, is overcome with the suburban blues of boredom. Though a university graduate herself, in fine arts, Emma has forfeited an artistic career due to the fact that her studio master and teacher, Jack Nadow, expected more from her than art. The realization that one of the unacknowledged lithographs in his collection of published works was in reality hers brings to the surface her supressed frustration and anger. These trigger a series of reactions which on a first reading could be understood as a play on stereotypical female hysteria where Emma, on the lines of Bovary, searches for excitement through greater social and sexual freedom. In reality, a closer reading discloses the manipulative hand of the author who, by subverting the narrative mode, puts into question not only a comparative analysis of the various Emma stories but even her own seemingly subjective rendering of Aida's past and present situation.

Though born in Germany after the Russian invasion of her homeland, Aida, upon arrival in the United States as a child, finds herself both displaced and without a sense of nation. Her father's house in Brooklyn becomes the official meeting place of Latvian exiles whose horror stories, political arguments and rowdy drinking binges irritate Aida and alienate her from the community. Their old world stories – where "there were no reasons, no choices, no consequences... The innocent and the wicked were both slaughtered"(94) – are symetrically opposed to the world and stories of Jane Austen where "moral choices were important; they had consequences. Words had meanings, shared and agreed to meanings" (94). Aida initially takes refuge from her cultural wilderness in Austen's fictive world and, later, married and living in Canada, in Flaubert's. But what slowly emerges is that even Edwards, with her continual questioning into the diverse creative processes of these two authors, takes refuge herself in the world of her own creation. She creates herself as omniscient narrator, and physically puts herself into the text in italics, commenting on her own act of writing, her interruptions like Austen's when guests or children call, at times even too tired with tedious household minutae to sit at the computer and write. As her own character Emma takes shape, she distances herself from Flaubert, who appears too detached, meticulous, sarcastic, and exacting in his fastidious dislike for Bovary's stupidity and illusions. She questions Flaubert's relationship to his Emma while trying to understand her own. "I watch my Emma," she writes, "but not from above . . . I know that stupidities often flow from my mouth, though I hope less frequently from my pen"(109). At the same time, she wishes to be like Flaubert in his capacity to use words and in his desire for artistic perfection. The author-narrator finds herself at grips with the tension between herself as creator and the feelings of anxiety about the world she has created. Her world of fiction fuses into other worlds of fiction which fuse into worlds of reality to foreground the collectiveness of experience of all modern day Emmas, whether they be young girls, housewives, artists, or writers. As underlined by the narrator, "I know that Emmas are not just around us, reader, Emma, *c'est nous*" (109).

At the end of the novel, Aida realizes that even her own love affair with Robert Lamartine was squalid like Bovary's, but she is given the choice to return to her husband, to her "other" and real self, not on the point of death but alive to the possibilities of her regained cultural identity. She recovers her relationship with her family, especially her mother, with her abandoned language, and with her artistic career. In this light, Aida finally represents the new generation of many Canadian ethnic women, the preservers of the "mother tongue," the archeologists of the past, but also the disseminators for a future grounded in hope and understanding

Like Monet's paintings, which are "not just about the going and coming of light but the experience of consciousness" (191), so Edwards' novella does not just comment on ethnic or feminist concerns, for what surfaces are the muted stories of modern day Emmas who, like Aida, would have "wanted to make lithographs and prints," would have wanted to succeed, but unfortunately felt the female encoding of not being "serious enough or strong enough or American enough or original enough" (153).

Dialogue

Caterina Edwards in conversation with Jacqueline Dumas

CATERINA EDWARDS: Both of us grew up with one language at home and another outside of home. That resulting sense that there are different ways of saying things, even different ways of seeing things, has been essential to both of our writing. I was always suspicious of one truth, one way.

JACQUELINE DUMAS: Me too. Maybe it is because both your parents and mine were first-generation immigrants (in my case Francophone). I write in English, but I have that sense that each word is important. Growing up with more than one language pushes you to examine each word. Like Beckett who wrote succinctly because writing in French made him consider each word that he put down. You are aware of how words can be misinterpreted. Speaking more than one language makes you privileged, because you have more than one view of the world, since language is not separate from culture. It is a way of seeing and being in the world. And being aware of more than one way of being is so valuable for a writer. It feeds your imagination.

CE: Exactly. That experience of two languages can also make you aware of the difficulty of all communication. You have been asked why you don't write in French. Why don't you?

JD: I don't because my environment is English. I have lived most of my life in English, so I am much more comfortable using it. If I lived in Quebec or France, after five or six years I would probably start writing in French. But now it is more natural for me to write in an English that is informed by my French background, with echoes of French, because that is who I am.

CE: My Italian wouldn't be good enough to write in Italian unless I lived there for a long stretch. Though I would be interested in doing translations from Italian.

JD: It was important to me, particularly in the first novel, to capture the French cadence. In your play and first novel, there is a definite Italian cadence.

CE: When I first started studying Italian literature, I got the sense that I didn't really know Italian. Also, when I was in Italy and I spoke Italian, especially in Sicily, friends often corrected the way I say things. But then, when I began to read more, I realized that I was actually not speaking incorrect Italian, but Venetian. I can also understand Istro-Veneto that is spoken in Istria, and which is on the UNICEF list of official endangered languages. Now I am more conversant with standard Italian, but still if I am not careful, I merge the languages.

JD: When I hear a French expression, I am not sure if it is an Alberta expression or one that I heard my French grandparents use or if it is from Montreal or Paris. When I am in France, people think I am French but they can't place me, they can't decide where I am from. I have my mother's accent, which is French, but I have a Canadian vocabulary. Two of my grandparents were from different parts of France, one from the North, the other from Savoie, and the other set was from Quebec, a real mishmash. Everyone knows that I am not from here, wherever here is. That's my identity.

CE: What a great line. As writers, both of us focus on characters that feel that they don't quite belong, wherever they are. Yet we both also try to remain connected to our respective "mother tongues." You keep up with reading contemporary writers in French. Do you find that reading in French influences the way you write in English?

JD: Definitely. One interviewer detected the influence of Anne Hébert, and I had been unconscious of it, but, as soon as he said it, I realized that it was true. She had influenced me. And I was pleased, because I respect and love her writing.

CE: I find that I do more and more reading in Italian and that I get more and more pleasure out of it. I had a wonderful time reading writers from Trieste, which is a very multicultural city. It interested me to see how writers who were part of an ethnic minority wrote in Italian. But I found the greatest affinity with Enrico Palandri, who writes in Italian but lives in Scotland. His novel, *La Via del ritorno* (The Way of the Return), tells of a return of a doctor who left Italy during the time of terrorism, the so-called years of lead in the 1970s, and is very concerned with the themes of immigration and *Italianità*. Palandri uses the structure of the train ride from London to Rome to order the book. I found that moving since, all through my childhood, my mother and I rode that train; we returned in just that way. So I knew each one of the stops, the scenes outside the windows. But what surprised me were his sentences. I felt that the rhythm in his sentences and what he was trying to achieve with those sentences was the same as the rhythm in and the will behind my sentences. (Though he wrote in Italian and I in English.) Reading his book, I felt an intense shock of recognition.

JD: In terms of cultural discordance, one of the things I notice in your writing, particularly in *The Lion's Mouth*, is a sense of the disintegration of the old and, at the same time, a sense of the ugliness of the new.

CE: Yes, it is there, with an attendant sense of frustration and loss. *[Laughing.]*

JD: And not knowing what to put in the place of the old or the ugly. The Canada you describe in your writing is not a sentimentalized nature. It's more that ugly West Edmonton mall, imitation of everything.

CE: My observations are not fair, are they?

JD: I'm not sure if they are fair or not. The point is that it is the Canada that your characters find. Where do you see yourself in that?

CE: I think I have a sense of Canada beyond West Edmonton mall, not just in the splendors of nature but in the beauty of cities like Vancouver or old Montreal.

JD: But neither of us describes that sort of city in our books. Maybe that is because we both feel that at least part of the role of the writer is to make the reader think, that our job is to make people question, to question ourselves, to question our society, to question our assumptions. Our job is both to develop our imagination and to help stimulate our reader's imagination and sensitivity to beauty.

CE: Calvino says that literature is necessary to politics "when it gives voice to whatever is without a voice, when it gives a name to what is without a name." Literature can touch on all that is excluded or repressed in both the individual and society. It is not the only purpose of literature, but still an important one.

JD: Yes, exactly. What I try to do in my writing is to clarify rather than obscure. And that is not the same as being simplistic.

CE: Not at all. In *Six Memos for the Next Millennium*, Calvino refers to the quality of lightness in literature, which he explains as a type of clarity. He also stresses the need for multiplicity. Lightness, quickness, exactitude, consistency, visibility, and multiplicity,

JD: Calvino's *Six Memos* is such a perceptive book. And a useful one.

CE: In *The Last Sigh*, Isabella, who has rejected Canada, says all sorts of nasty things about Canadians. How mean spirited they are underneath the niceness.

JD: Yes, I think there is a real myth about our niceness. We have this idea of ourselves: we are not Americans and not racist and not this and that. That idea denies so much. And our stories of our parents and grandparents coming and breaking the land ignore the real story: that there were already people here.

CE: It also ignores how glorified their toils were.

JD: People came thinking they had to make a mini-Europe, and they brought their prejudices with them, and their darkness. We are hypocritical as a people. We don't want to look at our dark side. We try to reap benefits without paying for them. Besides, I find it more interesting to explore those things rather than just accept all the myths.

CE: We are back to your point that our job as writers is to question. I noticed in *Madeleine and the Angel*, in terms of cultural discordance, that your character Maria Goretti remains more connected to her ethnic background, her Frenchness than Pauline, her sister. Pauline rejects that community because she connects it to her parents.

JD: That's right. The only way she can find herself is to reject everything and start anew. It is almost like a positive disintegration.

CE: So we are both concerned with the process of disintegrating and starting again. Rereading your novel I felt emotionally that Maria Goretti and Pauline function as different sides of the same person. Even though they have a different approach to their French background.

JD: That's exactly right. The way the father is both the angel and the devil.

CE: Eli Mandel wrote an article once on how doubles are a particular concern of ethnic writers.

JD: Certainly. In *The Lion's Mouth*, for example, Marco is Bianca's dark twin, her Italian side.

CE: An ineffectual one.

JD: Morally and emotionally weak. He literally has no stomach.

CE: Hard not to read that symbolically. You read an academic article on the prevalence of doubleness in the work of writers that feel connected to two cultures, and you think that it has nothing to do with you and your writing. You certainly don't plan on using doubles. But they can still be there.

JD: Speaking of that cultural duality, I was amused when I was reading *The Lion's Mouth* where you have Marco, the architect, opposing the new complex-resort on the Lido. But then Raponi wears cologne that smells of pine trees, as he wants to demolish everything in sight yet bottle the outdoors. That came from Canada, the pine trees.

CE: But it's an artificial scent. Another thing that we have in common is that we both write about Maria Goretti and her influence.

JD: When we were young she was the main saint held up for us to emulate. I was worried when I was a child that I would be attacked as she was. And what would my choice be? Would I be brave enough to die rather than submit?

CE: I was pretty sure I wouldn't be brave enough. What

I didn't see then that I see now was that she was a child, she was eleven.

JD: You often have male characters who take out their frustration in violence. Your female characters don't. They tend to be verbal, capable, efficient. The men are ambiguous, confused, and as I mentioned before, weak, though physically strong.

CE: The novel I'm working on now has the same pattern: a weak man and a capable and strong wife. (He can't adjust to a new country while she is a success at forging a new life.) But I don't know where that pattern comes from. I don't think I see all male and female relationships in that light. I hope not.

JD: In *The Lion's Mouth* you have a scene with French Canadians in a small Venetian shop and they take up so much space. It is an interesting detail, because there is a real difference. A Spanish person is compact and takes up very little space. In North America we have big bodies and spread ourselves out. We aren't aware of how we use up other people's space.

CE: Sometimes in Europe, I feel that I don't have enough space.

JD: In many of your scenes, like the family meal at Tarquinio's, everyone is playing a role. You seem to be saying that people here are allowed more freedom in their roles.

CE: I think they do have more freedom here. I think people in Italy do break out of their roles, but it involves more of a struggle because the family is so strong, and your position in the family is so important.

JD: I see that as a thread all through your work. The importance of breaking out of roles, breaking out of the predictable, away from what is expected of you.

CE: Yes, I don't think I have entirely succeeded at breaking out in my life.

JD: Although you stress that Italians are bound by their tradition, in *The Lion's Mouth* Bianca says that there are traditions here that bind the writer. If you grow up on the prairies, you are expected to write about your struggle against your environment.

CE: Traditions and received ideas bind us here, but we aren't as conscious of them.

JD: We like to see ourselves as hopeful.

CE: I have found that there is an angry response if you suggest that things here aren't perfectly egalitarian. Or that writers from different classes, races, or regions don't have equal access to the mainstream press. Critics point out that many ethnic writers have become very successful. Which is certainly true. But an ethnic writer is most likely to be welcomed into the mainstream if they present an image of another country that confirms what the Canadian reader already thinks of that country. A writer from India who stresses the exoticism, the heat, the dust, the poverty, and the crowds becomes better known internationally than the one who writes about the "middle-class." It is still difficult for a writer to be accepted if he or she presents a new, different view, breaking the stereotypes.

JD: You don't think things have changed that way?

CE: Things have gotten better. *The Lion's Mouth* came out in 1982, before ethnic writers became fashionable. If it had portrayed an Italy that was primitive, peasants and poverty and wise tales, with lots of tomato sauce and garlic, it would have been more successful. We may have won a few skirmishes, but not the war.

JD: It is like feminism; the problems are still there, so how can we speak of post-feminism?

CE: There are too many expectations of what Italian-Canadian writing should be both on the part of Canadian and Italian critics. When my play, *Homeground*, was being considered for production in other cities, several directors considering the play commented that the characters should not be so articulate. I thought that was so condescending. They thought that as immigrants they should be speaking in broken English or with that stereotyped "Italian" accent.

JD: My publisher was surprised to find that *Madeleine and the Angel* was perceived as not being of interest to a Quebec audience. In the publishing world, the perceived view is that the Quebecers have no interest in reading about the Francophone experience in Alberta because, of course, we don't exist. St. Boniface, Moncton, and that's about it. *[Laughter.]* As René Lévèsque said, we're dead ducks.

CE: All Italian-Canadian writers should live in Toronto.

JD: We are still up against these myths.

CE: I suspect that *The Lion's Mouth* being published with a small, Western regional press, while it was so much about Italy and being Italian-Canadian, that hurt the book. But isn't that true for you too? Especially for *The Last Sigh* which has a strong international appeal and is set in Granada.

JD: *The Last Sigh* was published by Fifth House, a small Saskatchewan press. I think the book was perceived as not what they should be publishing. They had trouble promoting that book. If Random House or another larger press had published it, it might have been different. Regional presses have the same problems as regional writers in terms of getting attention nationally or internationally. The trend in the publishing industry now is that proven popular writers are getting their books published and marketed. And every publisher seems to be looking for the new, young and photogenic writer. But writers who have two or three books out are really having trouble being published. What happened to nurturing a writer? Big box bookstores and big box publishers are looking for the big box sellers. A sorry trend.

CE: Because it is so homogenizing, so predictable. In publishing, there are expectations of who should be writing what and how you should do it.

JD: Writers now are expected to market the book. So publishers are buying the personality instead of the work.

CE: When I was trying to place my new book, *Deadly Elements*, different publishers expressed doubt about how they would market the book. They seemed confused because it is both a mystery and a literary novel. Editors wanted it to fit into one box or the other. I don't think they would have cared if I were a big name.

JD: Writers are asked to write marketing proposals. Everything has to be looked at as a business, even universities. But it is a terrible way to approach art. It is all part of the Americanization of culture.

CE: I do think it has a dampening effect on what is produced. You are punished for not fitting into a restrictive slot.

JD: Don't even try to be experimental, cutting edge. One of the real differences between North America and Europe is the status of the artist. In Spain I was respected because I was a writer, not in spite of it. That was my place in society.

CE: I had a similar experience when I was writing *The Lion's Mouth*. I was welcomed wherever I went in Venice and could ask any questions I wanted because I was a writer. I hadn't published a book at that point, but I was still treated with respect. Not here. I think the attitude here partly comes from the romantic image of the artist as outlaw. Instead, as an artist, you are a part of the society; you are neither better nor worse than anyone else is.

JD: Here you are respected if you have sold a lot of books. If you are not being bought, you have no value. You aren't considered a success because you have opened people's eyes or made them think a different way. Or have introduced beauty into their world. I think it also relates to the pioneering background of this province. Art is still seen as a frill.

CE: That is the attitude of most immigrants too. What matters is making as much money as possible. Having the best house.

JD: We are overgeneralizing, of course. But the people who settled here often lost more than their culture. They lost the idea of culture.

CE: You mentioned I refer to art a great deal in my work. I do because I believe in the importance of art. The memory of the Etruscan statues in *Whiter Shade of Pale* causes the narrator to question his life. Those statues say that what is essential to a good relationship between a man and a woman is equality, tenderness, and courtesy. Art from a distant time can still speak to you now.

JD: But politicians seem to think that art can only say what they want it to say, that it should glorify our society as it is. But fiction is one of the best ways to question.

CE: You said you had different experiences being interviewed by the French and English language media.

JD: I did. In the English interviews in the radio station, you sat across a wide table, the atmosphere was very cold, and then the interviewer asked very personal questions about my mother and whether particular incidents in the book had really happened. In the interviews for the

French language media, the interviewer would sit very close and come across in a warm and intimate manner. But the questions were not invasive; they were about the novel, about style and substance. My first novel deals with sexual violence and physical violence. I carefully wrote it so it had no specific, voyeuristic details. Sometimes I had the impression that the English media would have liked me to break down on air. They would have liked me to come up with those kinds of details. Most of them weren't interested in the novel itself.

CE: We are back to having to sell ourselves. If you cry or express intense emotions, you are a saleable author.

JD: One national radio program decided not to interview me when I told them I would not talk about my personal life.

References

Italo Calvino, *The Uses of Literature*, p.98

Italo Calvino, *Six Memos for the Next Millennium.* Harvard U. P. 1988.

Eli Mandel, "The Ethnic Voice in Canadian Writing," in *Figures in a Ground.* Saskatoon, 1978.

A Brief Biography of Caterina Edwards

Caterina Edwards' background is Italian, Croatian, Welsh, and English. Frank Edwards was an English soldier stationed in Venice, Italy, right after World War II. The Royal Engineers of the British Army requisitioned the house where Rosa Pagan and her two sisters were living. Frank and Rosa later married and moved to Wellingborough, England, where Caterina was born in 1948, as part of the Welsh and English family. In 1956 Caterina's parents emigrated to Canada, and she grew up in Calgary, attending the local Catholic schools. Since Caterina's mother had six brothers and sisters back in Venice she sent her there to spend several summers with her aunts. She learned that her Venetian grandfather, Renato Pagan, had moved to Dalmatia where he met and married a Croatian woman, Caterina Letich, her grandmother. By the time she reached university, Caterina had strong links with Venice and a sense of her diverse ethnic roots. See her essay, "Where the Heart Is."

From Calgary she went to Edmonton to enroll at the University of Alberta, but her concerned parents had her live with a local Italian family, Pietro and Ausilia Contessa. Even though she was away from home attending a very Canadian university she was still linked to the Italian immigrant community, an experience which is reflected in her later writing. In 1970 she earned an honours B.A. in English literature. The university had several active Canadian writers on staff in this decade: novelists, Henry

Kreisel, Sheila Watson and Rudy Wiebe along with poets, Dorothy Livesay, Wilfred Watson, Douglas Barber, Stephen Scobie, and E.D. Blodgett. For several years Caterina had developed an interest in writing and so she enrolled in the masters program in creative writing. After working with Rudy Wiebe and Sheila Watson she earned an M.A. in 1973. Her first published story was, "The Last Young Man," which appeared that year in *The Journal of Canadian Fiction*.

In the meantime she had met and married Marco Lo Verso, an American student of Italian background who had grown up in Sacramento, California. Marco earned a Ph. D. in English literature and began teaching at Concordia University College in Edmonton. Caterina began to teach English at Grant MacEwan Community College. She continued to publish short stories in literary journals such as *Branching Out* and *Dandelion*. Her story, "Everlasting Life," was included in Rudy Wiebe's anthology, *Getting Here* (1977), one of the first books printed by NeWest Press of Edmonton. In 1980 Rudy Wiebe and Aritha van Herk edited the important anthology, *More Stories from Western Canada* and included Edwards' "The Island of the Nightingales," which has become one of her signature stories along with "Prima Vera."

With the publication of her first novel, *The Lion's Mouth*, in 1982, Edwards became the first Canadian writer to explore the life of an Italian immigrant woman in Western Canada. This is the same year that Frank Paci brought out *Black Madonna*, a narrative about an Italian immigrant woman from Sault Ste. Marie in Northern Ontario. In the 1980s these two titles became the most popular novels adopted in university literature courses on the theme of immigration.

Edwards examined the life of Italian immigrants in the prairies in her first play, *Terra straniera*, which was a major success at the 1986 Edmonton Fringe Festival. The play was published under the title, *Homeground*. At this time Edwards was teaching creative writing at the University of Alberta, and continuing to publish short stories.

She was literary editor for *Il Caffè: International Journal of the Italian Expereince*. She is active in the Alberta Writers' Guild and has served on the executive of the Association of Italian-Canadian Writers which was founded in 1986.

With the publication of her two novellas, *Whiter Shade of Pale/ Becoming Emma* (1992), Edwards demonstrated her continuing interest in narrative forms. Life writing is the focus of *Eating Apples: Knowing Women's Lives* (1994), an anthology which she edited with Kay Stewart of the University of Alberta. Her later books are evidence of her desire to challenge the narrative conventions in Canada. Her influence as a teacher of creative writing has continued to expand with her tutoring at Athabasca University, a distance education institution with students all over North America.

The life of Caterina Edwards is a delicate balance between life and art. Caterina and Marco have raised their two daughters, Tatiana and Antonia, to speak Italian. They visit Italy as often as they can and have spent whole summers in Venice.

Bibliography

WORKS BY AND ABOUT CATERINA EDWARDS

BOOKS

The Lion's Mouth. Edmonton: NeWest Press, 1982.
_____. New Edition. Montreal: Guernica Editions, 1993.
La Gueule du lion. (Fr. trans. Jocelyne DoRay) Montreal: Editions Balzac, 2000.
Homeground (a play). Montreal: Guernica Editions, 1990.
Whiter Shade of Pale / Becoming Emma (two novellas). Edmonton: NeWest Press, 1992.
Island of the Nightingales (short stories). Toronto: Guernica Editions, 2000.

ANTHOLOGIES

Eating Apples: Knowing Women's Lives. Edited with Kay Stewart. Edmonton: NeWest Press, 1994.
Wrestling with the Angel: Women Reclaiming their lives. Edited with Kay Stewart. Red Deer: Red Deer College Press, 2000.

SHORT STORIES

"The Last Young Man," *Journal of Canadian Fiction*, II, 2 (Spring, 1973), 25-28.
"All Life from the Sea," *Branching Out*, (March/April, 1974).
"Everlasting Life," *Getting Here*. ed. Rudy Wiebe. Edmonton: NeWest Press, 1977.
"Full Moon," *The Story So Far 5*. Toronto: Coach House Press, 1978.
"Frost King," *Dandelion*, VII, 2 (1980).
"Island of the Nightingales," *More Stories form Western Canada*. eds. Rudy Wiebe and Aritha van Herk. Toronto: Macmillan of Canada, 1980.
_____. *Italian Canadian Voices: An Anthology of Poetry and Prose*. ed. Caroline M. DiGiovanni. Oakville: Mosaic Press, 1984.
"Quirks and Quarks," *Double Bond*. Saskatoon: Fifth House, 1985.
"Prima Vera," *Alberta Bound*. ed. Fred Stenson. Edmonton: NeWest Press, 1986.

_____. *Ricordi: Things Remembered*. ed. C.D. Minni. Montreal: Guernica, 1989.

"Master of Arts," *The Best of Alberta*. eds. Tom Radford & Harry Savage. Edmonton: Hurtig Publishing, 1987.

"Backwater," *Il Caffè: International Journal of Italian Experience*. VII, 1 (March/April, 1987).

_____. *The Anthology of Italian-Canadian Writing*. ed. J. Pivato. Toronto: Guernica Editions, 1998.

"Stella's Night," *Alberta ReBound*. ed. Aritha van Herk. Edmonton: NeWest Press, 1990.

_____. *Pillars of Lace: The Anthology of Italian-Canadian Women Writers*. ed. M. De Franceschi. Toronto: Guernica Editions, 1998.

"Home and Away," *Other Voices*, 5, 1 (Spring, 1992).

"On a Platter," *Boundless Alberta*. ed. Aritha van Herk. Edmonton: NeWest Press, 1993.

"Loving Italian," *The Toronto Review of Contemporary Writing Abroad*. 16, 3 (Summer, 1998).

Chapters 9, 10 & 15 of *The Lion's Mouth* in *Pillars of Lace*, op. cit.

> A number of stories were broadcast on regional and national radio.

Essays

"A Playwrght's Experience," *Writers in Transition*. eds. C. D. Minni and Anna Foschi Ciampolini. Montreal: Guernica Editions, 1990.

"Discovering Voice: The Second Generation Finds Its Place," *Italian Canadiana*, II (Spring 1996).

"Sublimation and Satisfaction: the Pains and Pleasures of the Autobiographical Impulse in Italian-Canadian Writing," *The Canadian Vision*. eds. Alessandro Anastasi, Giovanni Bonanno and Rosalba Rizzo. Messina: Edizioni Officina Grafica, 1996.

"Care Calling Care," *Eating Apples: Knowing Women's Lives*. Edmonton: NeWest Press, 1996.

"From Sea to C Minus," *Memoria e Sogno: Quale Canada Domani?* eds. Giulio Marra, Anne De Vaucher, and Alessandro Gebbia. Venice: Supernova, 1996.

"Where the Heart Is," *True North: Canadian Essays for Composition*. ed. Janice Macdonald. Don Mills: Addison-Wesley, 1999.

"Under My Skin," *Going Some Place: Anthology of Creative Non-Fiction*. ed. Lynn Van Luven. Regina: Coteau Books, 2000.

"Where the Heart Is," *Palinsesti Culturali: Gli apporti delle immigrazioni alla letteratura del Canada*. eds. Anna Pia De Luca, J.P. Dufiet, A. Ferraro. Udine: Forum, 1999.

Caterina Edwards has given a number of conference papers in North America and Europe.

Publications About the Work of Caterina Edwards

Bishop, Ted. "Cave and Crystal," *Canadian Literature* 102 (1984).

Clement, Lesley. "Two Returns," *Canadian Literature* 136 (1993).

De Luca, Anna Pia. "The Death of Illusion in Caterina Edwards'*The Lion's Mouth*," in *Cross-Cultural Studies: American, Canadian and European Literature, 1945-1985*. ed. Mirko Jurak. Ljubljana: University of Ljubljana, 1988.

_____. "La Scrittura etnica in Canada: due mondi a confronto," *Rivista di Studi Canadesi*, 6 (1993), 37-51.

Di Giovanni, Caroline M. "Italian Canadian Writers: Themes of the First Generation," *Canada Ieri e oggi*. ed. Giovanni Bonanno, Fasano: Schena Editor, 1985.

Fachinger, Petra. "Italianità," *Canadian Literature* 145 (Summer, 1995).

Minni, C.D. "The Short Story as an Ethnic Genre," *Contrasts*. ed. J. Pivato. Montreal: Guernica Editions, 1985.

Pivato, J. "The Return Journey in Italian-Canadian Literature," *Canadian Literature* 106 (Fall, 1985).

_____. "Italian-Canadian Women Writers Recall History," *Canadian Ethnic Studies*. XVIII, 1 (1986).

_____. "Constantly Translating: The Challenge for Italian-Canadian Writers," *Canadian Review of Comparative Literature*, XIV, 1 (March, 1987), 61-76.

_____. *Echo: Essays on Other Literatures*. Toronto: Guernica Editions, 1994.

Tuzi, Marino. *The Power of Allegiances*. Toronto: Guernica Editions, 1997.

Verdicchio, Pasquale. "The Borders of Writing," in *Devils in Paradise: Writings on Post-Emigration Cultures*. Toronto: Guernica Editions, 1997.

Theses

Bonato, Lisa. *Mothers and Daughters in Italian-Canadian Women's Literature.* M.A., Comparative Literature, University of Alberta, 1994.

Canton, Licia. *The Question of Identity in Italian-Canadian Fiction.* Ph.D. Études anglaises, Université de Montréal, 1998.

Fachinger, Petra. *Counter-Discursive Strategies in 'First World' Migration Writing.* Ph.D. Comparative Literature. University of British Columbia, 1993.

Padovan, Graziella. *Memorie Etniche e Strutture Metanarrative nei Romanzi di Joy Kogawa e Caterina Edwards.* M.A. Lingue e Letterature Germaniche e Romanze. Università di Udine. 1991.

Sarlo-Hayes, Elizabeth. *The Italian Immigrant Woman in Post World War II Canada: Overt and Covert Stories.* M.A. Canadian Studies. Trent University, 1997.

Sozzi, Graziella. *Dualismo Etnico e Scoperta di Sé* in *The Lion's Mouth* di Caterina Edwards. M.A. Lingue e Letterature Straniere. Università degli Studi di Catania. 1995.

Tuzi, Marino. *Identity, Multiplicity and Repesentational Strategies in Italian-Canadian Fiction.* Ph.D. English Literature. York University, Toronto, 1995.

List of Contributors

Frank Caucci has taught at McGill U. and Acadia U. and is presently Associate Professor of French and Canadian Studies at Indiana University Northwest. In addition to numerous articles on Canadian Literature he published *Les Voix d'éros: La Poésie amoureuse de Paul Éluard et Pablo Neruda*, as well as French translations of the poetry of Pier Giorgio Di Cicco, *Les Amours difficiles* (Guernica, 1990), and Mary di Michele (*Pain et chocolat*, Le Noroît, 1996). He is currently working on the third solitude in Canadian literature.

Anna Pia De Luca was born in Italy and grew up in Canada. She has degrees from the University of Toronto and now teaches English and Canadian literature at the University of Udine. She has published many articles on Canadian writers and has edited *Palinsesti culturali: Gli apporti delle immigrazioni alla Letteratura del Canada*. Udine, 1999.

Jacqueline Dumas was born in Alberta and has lived in Montreal, France, and Spain. She has published three books: *I'm Never Coming Back*, ill. Iris Paabo (Annick Press, 1986, a children's book), *Madeleine and the Angel* (Fifth House, 1989, Writers' Guild of Alberta First Novel Award), and *The Last Sigh* (Fifth House, 1993). She is the owner/manager of Orlando Books Ltd. an Edmonton bookstore which promotes Canadian authors.

Petra Fachinger has a Ph.D. (1993) in Comparative Literature from U.B.C. where she taught for some years. Since 1998 she has been Assistant Professor in German at Queen's University. Her publications include: "Werther's Others: From Plenzdorf to Pirinçci." *Seminar* 33.1 (1997), "Writing Back to the German 'Masters,.'" *Canadian Review of Comparative Literature* 24.2 (1997), and "Lost in Nostalgia: The Autobiographies of Eva Hoffman and Richard Rodriguez," *Melus*, (Winter, 1999).

Joseph Pivato was born in Italy, grew up in Toronto, and has a

Ph.D. in Comparative Literature from the University of Alberta. He teaches literature at Athabasca University and has published: *Contrasts* (1985), *Echo* (1994) and *The Anthology of Italian-Canadian Writing* (1998), all with Guernica.

Elizabeth Sarlo-Hayes did her M.A. in Canadian Studies at Trent University and now teaches school in North Bay, Ontario. Her M.A. thesis was on Italian-Canadian women writers.

Marino Tuzi was born in Italy, earned a Ph.D. in English from York University, and teaches Canadian Studies at Seneca College in Toronto. In addition to articles on Canadian writing he has published *The Power of Allegiances*, Guernica Editions, 1997.

Pasquale Verdicchio was born in Italy, raised in Canada, and has a Ph.D. in Italian Studies from UCLA and teaches at the University of California, San Diego. He has published several books of poetry and criticism including: *Devils in Paradise* (1997) and *Approaches to Absence* (1994). He has served as president of the Association of Italian-Canadian Writers.